Where Hearts Gather

Recipes, Memories, and Wisdom from Mom's Kitchen

Susan West Cannon

Special Delivery Publications
Lubbock, Texas

ISBN 1-885620-03-9

First Printing	December 1999	5,000
Second Printing	April 2001	3,000
Third Printing	January 2003	5,000

Cover designed by Dell Cannon
Antique print from private collection
Background pattern copyright F. Schumacher & Co. used with permission

Illustrations by Susan Cannon

Published by
Special Delivery Publications
5109 82nd Street, Suite 7, #204
Lubbock, Texas 79424-3099
1-800-533-8983
www.whereheartsgather.com

WIMMER
COOKBOOKS

ConsolidatedGraphics
1-800-548-2537

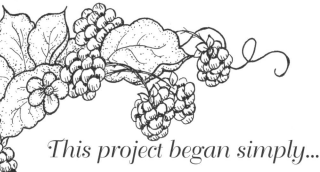

This project began simply...

After my mother-in-law, Naydiene, passed away, several family members wanted her recipes. If I had known then what I know now, I would have simply copied her recipe cards. Never doing things the easy way, I decided to write a cookbook using her recipes. Writing this book has taken me on a journey of sorts... going through recipes, collecting old family pictures, and remembering family gatherings, especially Sunday lunch with my in-laws, Otis and Naydiene. Finally, five years later, after hours of writing and cooking, (which my husband and kids loved) here is the final product.

It is more than a tribute to Naydiene, it is a tribute to the women in my life. My patient mother who first taught me to cook, to my grandmothers who shared their love for family, and my mother-in-law, Naydiene, who had that special gift for welcoming guests, making them feel like family, and preparing meals with ease.

These dear ladies inspired me, and it is my hope that they will inspire you to record your family recipes and stories. If your family does not have a tradition of eating together, be the one to start the tradition. Your family will be blessed!

Susan
Cannon

Special Thanks

This cookbook would not have been possible without my husband Dell. His creativity on the cover, patient typesetting and layout of the recipe pages, and his encouragement made this cookbook a reality. And to my children Logan and Kaitlyn, thank you for your enthusiasm and for being my taste testers.

Also to my sister, Karen, and Dell's cousin, Jeannie, thank you for continuing to ask when the cookbook would be ready! Special thanks must go to my dear friend, Cyndy Douglas, for her wonderful insight and encouragement and to my new friend, Twyla Stair, for her patient proofing!

Last but not least thank you to my mother, Jeanette West, for answering all of my questions, introducing me to chocolate chip cookies, and most of all for being my mom!

I would be remiss if I did not thank each of you that have shared recipes with our family. All of Naydiene's friends are wonderful cooks. I wish I could name each of you, but there are just too many! You lovely ladies and dear friends know how much Naydiene loved and appreciated you.

Many of the recipes have been part of our family for so long no one remembers exactly where they came from. So if one looks just like your recipe for.... just know that it has been enjoyed by our family and will be enjoyed for generations to come!

Contents

$\mathcal{N}$o matter where we go in search of success and happiness we always come back home. Home to the warmth and aroma of the family kitchen. Home to the comfort of gathering around the table. Home to the kitchen where kids drop their backpacks, where homework and special projects are completed, where we share our dreams and our fears, where we gather to share more than food... we gather to share our hearts and nourish our souls.

Appetizers &
Beverages

No matter where
I serve my guests
they seem to like my
kitchen best!

Pretty Plates and Life Lessons

When I first met my mother-in-law, Naydiene, I thought she was amazing. She was a great cook, her house was immaculate, she painted beautifully, and she was a gracious hostess. She made it all look so easy!

When it came to planning a meal or event, Naydiene thought of every detail. She spoke of things about which I had never thought. For example, I was planning a luncheon and Naydiene said, "Be sure you have a pretty plate." I thought, "Well of course I'll use my pretty dishes." However, through further conversation, I realized she was talking about the color and presentation of the *food,* not the plate it was served on! I watched all of this with awe, a feeling of inadequacy and a little... "Well this is the 80's and we work now. We just don't have time to worry about those things. We are career women."

Interestingly enough, Naydiene had been a career woman for a large portion of her life. She worked in a furniture store while her boyfriend, Otis Cannon, was off fighting in World War II. Later, after they married, she managed the silver department at Anderson Brothers Jewelers in Lubbock, but quit when her son Dell arrived.

It was obvious being a homemaker was what she loved. Her home and family were the most important "management positions" she had ever held. Thank goodness Naydiene was a patient teacher. Through the years I learned a lot about cooking, but even more about life.

-12-06 These are delicious!

Elegant Cream Cheese Stuffed Mushrooms
"Easy and delicious"

1½	pounds small fresh mushrooms
1	(8-ounce) package cream cheese, softened
dash	salt
dash	Worcestershire sauce
1	cup fresh grated Parmesan cheese
	fresh ground pepper to taste

Wash mushrooms well and remove stems. Drain well on paper towels. Combine remaining ingredients and mix well. Spoon mixture into mushroom caps. Place on a lightly greased baking sheet. Sprinkle with additional Parmesan. Bake at 350° for 20 minutes or until cheese mixture is beginning to lightly brown.

Yield: approximately 4 dozen

This is our favorite appetizer! Attractive and easy to make, they are always a hit with our guests!

Note: Wash the mushrooms just before you are ready to use them. Mushrooms tend to absorb water so you do not want to immerse them. Just quickly rinse under cold running water and drain on paper towels.

Appetizers

Served as an appetizer, this bread is also good with pasta and a salad. In fact, we like this bread so much we can make a meal out of it alone!

Olive-Cheese Bread

½	cup butter, softened
¼	cup Hellman's mayonnaise
1	teaspoon California-style garlic powder
1	teaspoon onion powder
2	cups grated Mozzarella cheese
½	cup finely chopped ripe olives
1	loaf unsliced French bread

Combine butter, mayonnaise, and seasonings. Stir in cheese and olives. Cut French bread in half lengthwise. Spread mixture on cut side of both halves of bread. Bake at 350° for 10 to 15 minutes or until cheese melts and edges of bread are lightly browned. Cut bread into slices, then cut slices in half. Delicious!

Southwestern Beef Crescent Rolls

1	pound ground beef
½	onion, finely chopped
1	teaspoon cumin
1	teaspoon oregano
1	teaspoon chili powder
½	teaspoon California-style garlic powder
2	tablespoons tomato paste
1	(8-ounce) carton sour cream
1	cup grated Monterey Jack cheese
	salt and pepper to taste
2	(8-ounce) cans refrigerated crescent roll dough

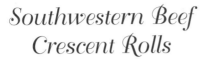 popular appetizer and so easy to make! The mild southwestern flavor makes these a favorite with all of our guests.

Brown ground meat, drain well. Add onions; sauté until onions are tender. Add remaining ingredients, except crescent roll dough. Heat mixture but do not boil. Remove from heat and let mixture cool somewhat. Unroll dough and separate into triangles. Cut each triangle in half lengthwise. Spread with mixture and roll up. Place rolls on lightly greased baking sheet. Bake at 375° for 12 to 15 minutes or until golden brown. Serve immediately.

Yield: 32 appetizers

Note: I have cooked the filling in the microwave. Just be sure to cook on medium after adding the sour cream.

Appetizers

An original recipe, this is the favorite of our household and all of our guests!

Note: I prefer to use a good quality brand of sour cream for this recipe. Choose a brand that is thick and creamy.

Always a favorite at our house, this queso is very filling because of the addition of the ground beef. If you would like to spice it up even more, use processed cheese with jalapenos in it.

Note: You can make this in your microwave.

Dell's Green Chile Dip

1	(16-ounce) carton sour cream
1	(7-ounce) can chopped green chilies, drained
1½	teaspoons seasoned salt
1	teaspoon California-style garlic powder
1	tablespoon chili powder
½	teaspoon cumin

Spoon sour cream into a bowl. (Note: Drain off any excess liquid.) Stir in green chilies and seasonings, mix until well blended. Chill before serving. This dip is best if made the morning or night before serving.

Queso

1	pound ground meat
1	package taco seasoning mix
⅓	cup water
1	(2-pound) box processed cheese spread
1	(10-ounce) can diced tomatoes with chilies

Brown ground meat. Drain well. Stir in taco seasoning and water. Cut cheese into cubes and place in top of double boiler; pour in tomatoes with chilies. Heat until cheese is melted. Stir ground beef into cheese mixture and simmer 3 to 5 minutes. Serve hot with tortilla or corn chips.

Guacamole

2	large ripe avocados
1	teaspoon California-style garlic powder
½	teaspoon salt
2	tablespoons minced onion
1	teaspoon seeded and minced jalapeno
2	tablespoons diced seeded tomato
	juice of ½ lime

Cut avocado in half, remove seed, and scoop out into a bowl. Mash with a fork. Stir in garlic powder and salt. Add remaining ingredients and stir until well combined. Serve immediately.

Note: This is great as a dip with white corn tortilla chips. It is also good in the recipe below.

Layer Dip

1	(8-ounce carton) sour cream
1	package taco seasoning mix
2	(10 ½ ounce) cans bean dip
1	recipe fresh guacamole
2	cups grated Cheddar cheese
½	cup diced green onion
2	cups coarsely chopped tomatoes
1	(3 ½-ounce) can diced ripe olives, drained

Combine sour cream and taco seasoning. Set aside. Layer bean dip, guacamole, sour cream mixture, then remaining ingredients. Chill and serve with assorted chips.

Appetizers

*T*his is one of Dell's specialties. He uses the type of avocados that have the bumpy skin and combines them with simple ingredients for an outstanding guacamole! Have your ingredients diced and ready to assemble but do not cut the avocado until right before serving. When exposed to air, the avocado will begin to turn brown. Some people say that placing the seed into the bowl of guacamole helps keep it from turning brown. This may work for awhile, but the guacamole will begin to turn dark. Guacamole is best when served fresh!

Appetizers

*D*on't wait for a special occasion to serve these. While they do make a good appetizer; they are also delicious with a bowl of soup or a salad.

Note: Store in an airtight container.

*A*nother classic Southern favorite that Naydiene often prepared. They can be made ahead of time and frozen. They do take a little extra time to make, but they are worth the effort.

Cheese Crisps

1	cup butter, softened
2	cups grated sharp Cheddar cheese
2	cups all-purpose flour
¼	teaspoon cayenne pepper
¼	teaspoon salt
2	cups crisp rice cereal

Combine butter, cheese, flour, cayenne, and salt in a large bowl; mix well. Slowly stir in rice cereal. Shape into walnut sized balls. Place on ungreased cookie sheet and flatten with a fork. Bake at 350° for 15 to 20 minutes.

Olive Cheese Balls

2	cups grated Cheddar cheese
1	stick butter, softened
1½	cups flour
½	teaspoon salt
2	tablespoons paprika
48	stuffed olives, well drained

Stir cheese and butter until well blended. Combine flour, salt, and paprika. Add to cheese/ butter mixture. Stir until well mixed. Roll dough around olives. Place on lightly greased baking sheet and bake at 400° for 15 minutes.

Yield: 48 appetizers

Hot Curried Crab Dip

½	pound King Crabmeat
1	(8-ounce) package cream cheese, softened
1	tablespoon Hellman's mayonnaise
¼	cup chopped green onions
2	tablespoons milk
1	tablespoon Worcestershire sauce
½	teaspoon curry powder
	salt and fresh ground pepper, to taste

Combine all the ingredients in top of double boiler and heat until mixture is hot. Stir until well blended. Transfer to a chafing dish and serve with assorted crackers or chips.

Another all-time favorite of our guests! Also easy to make. My husband's only complaint about this dip is that I don't make it often enough!

Note: You can soften your cream cheese in the microwave. Place unwrapped cream cheese in a microwave safe bowl and heat at 50% power for 45 seconds to 1 minute.

Hot Broccoli Dip

2	(10-ounce) packages frozen chopped broccoli
½	medium onion, diced
¼	cup butter or margarine
1	(10 ¾ ounce) can cream of mushroom soup
1	(6-ounce) roll garlic cheese

Cook broccoli until tender and drain well. Sauté onion in butter until soft. Add broccoli, soup, and cubed cheese. Stir and heat until well blended and cheese has melted. Serve hot in a chafing dish with chips.

A family favorite, this dip is especially good served with large corn chips.

15

Appetizers

A simple recipe and a simply wonderful appetizer. I love crescent rolls because you can quickly turn them in to so many delicious treats!

Bacon Sour Cream Crescents

1	(8-ounce) can refrigerated crescent roll dough
½	cup sour cream
½	teaspoon onion salt
½	pound bacon, cooked crisp, drained and crumbled

Unroll dough and separate into triangles. Spread each with sour cream and sprinkle with onion salt. Top with crumbled bacon. Cut each triangle into 3 equal wedges lengthwise. Roll up each wedge. Place on lightly greased baking sheet and bake at 375° for 12 to 15 minutes or until golden brown. Serve warm.

Yield: 24 appetizers

Easy to make and always a favorite. I prefer these when they are served hot and crisp just out of the oven!

Cannon Balls

1	pound sausage (hot or mild)
1	pound Cheddar cheese, grated
2	cups biscuit baking mix

Crumble and fry sausage; drain well. Combine cooked sausage, biscuit mix, and cheese; stir well. Form into walnut-sized balls. Place on ungreased cookie sheet and bake in a 350° oven for 10 to 15 minutes. Serve warm.

Note: Cannon Balls freeze well!

Fresh Fruit Dip

1   (8-ounce) package cream cheese, softened
1   (7-ounce) jar marshmallow creme
dash of cinnamon (optional)

Cream softened cream cheese until smooth; add marshmallow creme and mix until well blended. Serve with assorted fresh fruit.

Note: To quickly soften cream cheese, remove wrapper, place in microwave safe dish, and heat in the microwave on medium power for 30 seconds.

*A*nother easy favorite, this is one appetizer even the kids will enjoy! It also makes a nice addition to any buffet or party table. Choose a variety of fruits for a colorful presentation.

2/30/05

Easy Caramel Dip

"So easy and delicious served with sliced apples"

1   (8-ounce) package cream cheese, softened
1   cup brown sugar
1   tablespoon vanilla

Mix all ingredients together until creamy. Serve with sliced apples and be prepared to accept compliments.

Note: Serve with an assortment of crisp apple slices like Granny Smith, Red Delicious, or Gala. Leave the peeling on. It adds to the taste and makes an attractive plate with the different colors.

*T*his is one of those recipes that tastes so good, people will want the recipe; and yet, when you give it to them, they won't believe something this delicious can be so quick and easy!

Appetizers

My husband, Dell, loves these pecans! Their unique flavor is always a hit with guests during the holidays. I like to package them in festive containers and give them as gifts to friends and neighbors.

Naydiene's Barbeque Pecans

6	cups shelled pecan halves
½	stick butter, melted
2	teaspoons seasoned salt
¼	teaspoon onion salt
¼	cup Worcestershire sauce
2	tablespoons ketchup
2	teaspoons chili powder

Place pecans in a large, deep bowl. In a smaller bowl, melt butter and stir in remaining ingredients. Pour butter mixture over pecans and stir until well coated. In a covered dish, bake pecans for 20 minutes in a 300° oven. Next pour pecans out on a cookie sheet. Sprinkle with table salt. Reduce oven temperature to 200° and bake pecans for 10 to 15 minutes. Drain and cool on paper towels. Store in an airtight container.

Gala Pecan Spread

1	(8-ounce) package cream cheese, softened
2	tablespoons milk
1	(2½-ounce) jar sliced dried beef
¼	cup finely chopped green pepper
2	green onions, chopped
¼	teaspoon California-style garlic powder
¼	teaspoon seasoned salt
¼	teaspoon fresh ground pepper
1	teaspoon Worcestershire sauce
½	cup sour cream
½	cup coarsely chopped pecans
2	tablespoons butter or margarine, melted
½	teaspoon seasoned salt

A delicious appetizer, this is also a nice change of pace from always serving a cheese ball.

Note: Use a glass pie plate or an attractive baking dish to cook this in since you do serve it directly out of the dish.

Combine softened cream cheese and milk, stir until well mixed. Chop dried beef; stir into cream cheese mixture along with the green pepper, green onions, seasonings, and Worcestershire sauce. Mix well. Fold in sour cream. Spread mixture in an 8-inch pie plate or baking dish. Heat the pecans in melted butter and seasoned salt until lightly browned. Spoon pecans on top of cream cheese mixture and bake in a 350° oven for 20 minutes. Serve hot with assorted crackers.

Appetizers

*T*wo yummy dips to serve with vegetables! This is a great way to provide a healthy and delicious appetizer. By choosing a variety of colorful veggies you can add color to your table. Be creative, serve the dip in a hollowed-out purple cabbage or red bell pepper.

Quick Veggie Dip

1	(3-ounce) package cream cheese, softened
⅓	cup sour cream
¼	cup ketchup
½	teaspoon prepared mustard
2	tablespoons chopped green onions

Mix ingredients in a small bowl until well blended. Chill. Serve with assorted veggies.

Party Vegetable Dip

1	(8-ounce) package cream cheese, softened
1	(4-ounce) package cream cheese, softened
⅓	cup chili sauce
½	cup mayonnaise
½	teaspoon Worcestershire sauce
⅓	cup finely chopped green onions, tops and bottoms
½	teaspoon seasoned salt

Combine all ingredients in a bowl and stir until well blended. Chill. Spoon into a hollowed-out head of purple cabbage and serve with assorted raw vegetables.

Deviled Eggs

6	hard boiled eggs
½	teaspoon salt
¼	teaspoon pepper
¼	teaspoon prepared mustard
2 to 3	tablespoons mayonnaise
dash	cayenne pepper

Cut boiled eggs in half lengthwise. Scoop out yolks, place in a bowl, and mash with a fork. Add remaining ingredients, adding mayonnaise until mixture is creamy. Refill whites with egg yolk mixture; heaping it up slightly. Chill.

Variation: Leave out cayenne pepper, add ¼ teaspoon sweet pickle relish and sprinkle eggs with paprika.

To boil eggs: Place eggs in saucepan; cover with cold water. Bring water to a boil; boil 6 minutes. Remove from heat; cover pan and let sit covered for 15 minutes.

Hint: Cut a thin slice off the bottom of each egg before filling so that once filled the eggs won't tip over.

Deviled eggs always remind me of family reunions and picnics. When my mother's family came together for the Bailey reunion in Arkansas, I could always count on there being deviled eggs among the many dishes of lovingly prepared food. Each year when Easter came around, the West family came together for our annual Easter picnic. As usual, there was an assortment of food, and thankfully, someone would always bring deviled eggs. Now, when I bite into one, memories of family and childhood come rushing back to me. What sweet memories!

Beverages

*T*his punch has been served at more family open houses, anniversary parties, and receptions than any other. It is always a favorite!

Hint: When you freeze the fruit mixture, divide it in half or thirds. That way it will be easier to mix consistent portions of frozen punch and lemon-lime drink, thus taking the guess work out of refilling your punch bowl and less stress for you, the hostess!

Banana Crush Punch

4	cups sugar
6	cups water
1	(46-ounce) can pineapple juice
2	(12-ounce) cans orange juice concentrate, thawed
1	(12-ounce) can frozen lemonade, thawed
6	bananas
6	(28-ounce) bottles lemon-lime beverage, chilled

Combine sugar and water; heat over low heat stirring until sugar is dissolved. Let cool. Purée bananas in blender and mix with thawed juices. (Do this immediately after puréeing banana to prevent purée from turning dark.) Combine mixture with sugar-water. Freeze until firm. To serve, thaw for 30 minutes; add lemon-lime beverage right before serving.

Yield: 60 servings

Note: Ginger ale may be used in place of the lemon-lime drink.

Karen's Favorite Punch

1 (64-ounce) bottle cranberry juice, chilled
1 (6-ounce) can frozen orange juice
1 (6-ounce) can pineapple juice
2 pints raspberry sherbet
1 (2-liter) lemon-lime beverage, chilled

Place frozen juices into punch bowl; gradually pour in cranberry juice and begin to break frozen juices apart. Continue to gently stir until mixture is slushy. Just before serving, add raspberry sherbet and chilled lemon-lime beverage.

Party Fruit Punch

2 (6-ounce) cans frozen lemonade
2 (6-ounce) cans frozen orange juice
1 (46-ounce) can pineapple juice
2 (3½-ounce) packages frozen strawberries
1½ cups sugar
2 (28-ounce) bottles ginger ale, chilled

Thaw juices and strawberries, combine with pineapple juice and sugar. Taste; add up to ½ cup more sugar for a sweeter punch. Freeze. Set out of freezer 30 minutes before serving. Pour chilled ginger ale over punch and serve.

Beverages

*M*y sister, Karen, serves this punch often because it is such a pretty punch and she receives so many compliments on it! Plus, it is very easy to make and requires little advance preparation.

*A*nother good party punch. Serve with an attractive ice ring. To make ice ring: arrange sliced oranges, lemons, and whole strawberries in bottom of a ring mold. Add just enough water to cover fruit (this will keep fruit from floating), freeze until firm. This will take about 4 to 5 hours. Fill remainder of mold with water and freeze.

Beverages

A summertime favorite with our kids! This is as pretty as it is delicious!

Cool and refreshing, this summertime favorite is a southern classic. Mint is one of the easiest herbs to grow! In fact, it grows so well it tends to "take over."

Cherry Lemonade

1 ½	cups sugar
½	cup water
	grated rind of one lemon
1 ½	cups fresh lemon juice
4 ½	cups ice water
⅓	cup Maraschino cherry juice

Place sugar and water in saucepan. Cook over low heat; stirring until sugar dissolves. Remove from heat; cool. Add lemon rind, lemon juice, and ice water. Stir well. Add cherry juice; stir. Serve over crushed ice.

Mint Tea

2	quarts water
4 to 5	family-size tea bags
1¼	cups sugar
4	fresh mint springs, washed
3	tablespoons lemon juice or juice of one lemon

In a large saucepan, bring water to a boil; add tea bags and mint leaves. Let simmer for 10 minutes. Remove tea bags, gently squeezing out water. Stir in sugar and lemon juice. Cook over low heat, stirring until sugar is dissolved. Strain mixture; cool. Serve over ice with a slice of lemon and a sprig of mint.

Favorite Hot Chocolate

¼	cup cocoa
½	cup sugar
⅓	cup hot water
	pinch of salt
4	cups milk
1	teaspoon vanilla extract

*N*othing warms you up on a chilly day like a cup of homemade hot cocoa!

Mix cocoa, sugar, water, and salt in a saucepan. Cook over medium heat, stirring constantly until mixture boils. Boil for 2 minutes, stirring continuously. Gradually stir in milk and heat thoroughly, but do not boil! Remove from heat; add vanilla. Serve immediately. Top with whip cream sprinkled lightly with cinnamon. Add a cinnamon stick stirrer and enjoy!

Almond Tea

*T*his is my favorite! It is also a very popular alternative to serve at a winter coffee or reception.

3	tablespoons instant tea
2	cups cold water
¾	cup sugar
2	cups hot water
2	small cans frozen lemonade, thawed
3	teaspoons vanilla
3	teaspoons almond flavoring
2	quarts water

Remember to warm your teapot by filling it with hot water. This takes the chill off so it will keep your tea warm longer.

Combine instant tea with cold water; set aside. In a large saucepan bring sugar and hot water to a boil; add tea mixture. Turn heat down and add thawed lemonade, vanilla, almond flavoring, and remaining water. Simmer. Serve hot.

Beverages

Wassail has been a Christmas Eve family tradition since my husband was a little boy. Naydiene always made sure there was hot Wassail ready and waiting to be enjoyed after their traditional Christmas Eve gift exchange.

The taste of this spiced cider is excellent, but an added benefit is the wonderful aroma that fills the house while it is simmering. Start your own Christmas tradition with Wassail or serve it at your next holiday open house!

Note: If you are having a large open house, this recipe is easy to double.

Wassail

2	quarts apple cider
½	cup sugar
1	teaspoon whole allspice
1	teaspoon whole cloves
1	(3-inch) cinnamon stick
½	lemon, thinly sliced
½	orange, thinly sliced

Combine cider and sugar in a large pan. Tie spices in a small piece of cheesecloth and place in pan with cider. Slowly bring to a boil, stirring occasionally. Reduce heat, add lemon and orange slices. Simmer for at least 15 minutes. Remove spice bag and serve hot.

Yield: 8 to 10 servings

Start a tradition: Serve this every year right after the family has decorated the Christmas tree. To make the event even more memorable serve the Wassail in special Christmas mugs. Years later, when your family sees the Christmas mugs they will be flooded with happy memories!

Breakfast & Breads

*A house is a home
when it shelters
the body
and comforts
the soul.*

P. Moffitt

A Heart for Hospitality

From the time I met Naydiene and married her son, I desired to cook as well as she did and entertain with the same ease. I continually rationalized that my generation was too busy, times were different, and you must be born with the gift of hospitality!

Then I had children of my own, and something kept nagging me. If I don't learn to do this who will pass it on to my daughter? Will my grandchildren miss out on the joy of family gatherings that I had experienced? Will they simply think you go to the local cafeteria or restaurant for Thanksgiving?! I wrestled with this for years and then one Sunday I was sitting in church and the preacher read Romans 12:10-13.

Be kindly affectionate to one another
with brotherly love,
in honor giving preference to one another;
not lagging in diligence, fervent in spirit,
serving the Lord; rejoicing in hope, patient in tribulation,
continuing steadfastly in prayer; distributing to the needs
of the saints, given to hospitality.

Hospitality? I suddenly woke up! I thought, "Wow, this is not something you are born with, it is a gift from God and it has more to do with your heart than your head!" If you have the desire and love for cooking and welcoming others into your home the gift of hospitality will follow. I left that day with a new perspective and I think for the first time I saw my role as a wife and mother more clearly. What I had searched to find, Naydiene had known all along. She was a good cook and gracious hostess because she loved what she was doing. It was not out of obligation or because of someone else's expectations. It was a gift of love from her heart!

Best-Ever Blueberry Muffins

Breakfast

2	sticks margarine, softened
¼	cup vegetable oil
2	eggs, beaten
1	cup canned blueberries with juice
1	cup buttermilk
5	cups sifted all-purpose flour
2	cups sugar
2	tablespoons baking powder
1	teaspoon baking soda
1	teaspoon salt
2	tablespoons Butavan flavoring

Combine margarine, oil, eggs, berries with juice, and buttermilk. Combine dry ingredients and gradually add to berry mixture; mix well. Stir in flavoring. Spray muffin pans with nonstick cooking spray. Fill cups ⅔ full of batter. Bake at 400° for 15 minutes or until lightly brown around edges. You can also use mini muffin pans; just cook for about 10 to 12 minutes.

Yield: 96 mini muffins or 32 regular size

Note: Butavan is a unique buttery flavoring found at bakeries and gourmet food stores. If you can't find it, simply do what my sister does; use 1 tablespoon vanilla and 1 tablespoon butter flavoring.

*T*hese are the best muffins! They are great for breakfast, or served as mini muffins with a meal.

Note: One 16 ½ ounce can of blueberries makes 2 batches of muffins. Be sure to spoon the blueberries out as you measure so you will get an even amount of blueberries and juice. Also, while you are baking, go ahead and make two batches. The extra muffins can be frozen in zip-top plastic freezer bags.

Grandmother's Coffee Cake

*F*riends and family will enjoy this flavorful coffee cake. Perfect for a brunch or coffee, this coffee cake is so good you will want to serve it often for your own family!

1	cup brown sugar, packed
1	cup white sugar
2	eggs
1	cup vegetable oil
1	teaspoon vanilla
2½	cups sifted flour
1	teaspoon cinnamon
1	teaspoon nutmeg
⅛	teaspoon salt
1	teaspoon baking powder
1	teaspoon baking soda
1	cup buttermilk
1	cup chopped pecans, lightly tossed in 2 tablespoons of flour
¾	cup coconut

Preheat oven to 350°. Beat sugars, eggs, oil, and vanilla until creamy. In a bowl combine flour, cinnamon, nutmeg, salt, baking powder, and soda. Alternately add the dry ingredients and buttermilk to sugar mixture. Blend well. Add flour-coated pecans and coconut. Bake in a greased and floured bundt pan for 45 to 50 minutes or until toothpick comes out clean. Cool in pan for 20 minutes.

Mom's Homemade Cinnamon Rolls

dough from Grammy's Roll recipe (page 39)
4   tablespoons butter, softened
¼   cup brown sugar
⅛   cup sugar
2   teaspoons cinnamon

Let dough rise in bowl. Punch down and place dough on floured work surface. Press into large rectangle. Spread softened butter on rectangle leaving ½-inch around the edge. Sprinkle with brown sugar, white sugar, and cinnamon. Starting with long edge, roll up and pinch seam to seal. Slice into 1½-inch sections. Place in a 9x13-inch baking dish that has been sprayed with nonstick cooking spray. Let rise. Bake at 325° for 20 to 25 minutes until golden brown. Drizzle glaze over warm rolls and serve.

Glaze:

1   cup powdered sugar
½   teaspoon vanilla
1½ to 2½ tablespoons milk

Combine all ingredients and stir until smooth.

Note: After placing rolls in pan, you can cover and refrigerate overnight or freeze up to a month. If frozen, allow rolls to thaw at room temperature then let rise in a warm oven before baking.

My mom, Jeanette West, makes these homemade cinnamon rolls almost every time we come to visit. The grandkids love them and so do the adults! Mom divides this recipe in half and makes two pans of cinnamon rolls. If your family is smaller, divide it in half and make one pan of cinnamon rolls and one pan of "Grammy Rolls." This way you have your breakfast and dinner rolls ready! My family likes large cinnamon rolls so I use this recipe and make one pan of cinnamon rolls. They have become a Christmas morning tradition at our house!

31

Breakfast

*D*elight your family with homemade buttermilk biscuits! Wonderful when served with your favorite jelly, or with sausage gravy for a hearty breakfast.

To make sausage gravy: After frying sausage, leave 2 tablespoons of drippings in the skillet. Add 2 to 3 tablespoons of flour and stir until it makes a thick paste. Brown flour mixture then slowly stir in 2 cups of milk. Continue stirring until gravy thickens and is bubbly. Add salt and pepper to taste. Serve hot over split biscuits. Note: you can add crumbled, cooked sausage to the gravy.

Buttermilk Biscuits

3	cups flour
2	tablespoons baking powder
½	teaspoon baking soda
2	tablespoons sugar
1	teaspoon salt
1	cup butter (cold, cut into pieces)
1¼	cups buttermilk

Preheat oven to 400°. In a large bowl sift dry ingredients together. Cut in butter with a pastry cutter until butter is in small pieces and mixture resembles rolled oats. Make a well in the center of the mixture and pour in buttermilk. Stir with a fork until combined (you may need to use your hands). Turn out onto a lightly floured workspace and roll out ½-inch thick. Cut into biscuits with medium size biscuit cutter. Place on a baking sheet that has been lightly sprayed with nonstick cooking spray. Place biscuits about 1 inch apart. Bake for 12 to 15 minutes until lightly browned.

Angel Biscuits

1	package dry yeast
¼	cup warm water
2½	cups flour
½	teaspoon baking soda
1	teaspoon baking powder
1	teaspoon salt
⅛	cup sugar
½	cup shortening
1	cup buttermilk

Light and airy, these biscuits have a smooth texture that will melt in your mouth!

Note: Dough can be refrigerated up to 3 days.

Dissolve yeast in warm water; set aside. Combine dry ingredients, cut in shortening. Stir in buttermilk and yeast mixture; mix thoroughly. To make biscuits, turn dough out onto floured surface and knead lightly. Roll out and cut with a biscuit cutter. Place biscuits on a cookie sheet that has been sprayed with nonstick cooking spray. Let rise slightly before baking. Bake in a 400° oven for 12 to 15 minutes or until golden brown.

Curried Fruit

1	(28-ounce) can peach halves
1	(28-ounce) can pear halves
1	(28-ounce) can apricot halves
1	(28-ounce) can chunk pineapple
1	stick butter, melted
1	cup brown sugar
1	tablespoon curry powder

An attractive and tasty dish to serve for breakfast or brunch, this fruit is especially good with ham, and makes a delicious side dish.

Drain all fruit well. Place fruit in a large, shallow pyrex dish. Melt butter, add brown sugar and stir until dissolved. Add the curry powder and a dash of salt. Pour mixture over fruit. Bake in a 350° oven for 30 to 40 minutes or until bubbly.

Breakfast

Sausage and Egg Casserole

A *favorite among our overnight guests, you can make this casserole ahead of time, refrigerate overnight, and bake the next morning.*

For variety substitute 2 cups of diced ham for the sausage. Add ⅓ cup of diced green pepper, ¼ cup of diced green onion, and ⅓ cup of sliced mushrooms. For spice add a 4-ounce can of green chilies!

1	(6-ounce) box of herb seasoned croutons
2	pounds bulk sausage
6	eggs
2½	cups milk
1	(10 ¾-ounce) can cream of mushroom soup
	salt and pepper to taste
2	cups grated Cheddar cheese

Preheat oven to 300°. Spray 8x8-inch baking dish with nonstick cooking spray. Cook sausage in a large skillet until brown, breaking up large chunks so sausage is crumbly. Drain sausage well on paper towels. Pour croutons in baking dish; spoon sausage over croutons. Beat eggs, milk, and mushroom soup together in a medium bowl. Add salt and pepper. Pour over sausage. Sprinkle cheese on top. Take a knife and marble cheese into egg mixture. Bake until set, approximately 1½ hours. Serve hot.

Yield: 6-8 servings

34

Mini Cream Cheese Cinnamon Rolls

1	tablespoon granulated sugar
2	tablespoons brown sugar
½	teaspoon cinnamon
1	(8-ounce) can refrigerated crescent rolls
2	ounces cream cheese, softened

Combine granulated sugar, brown sugar and cinnamon; set aside. Carefully unroll crescent roll dough and press together seams and perforations to make one complete rectangle of dough. Spread with softened cream cheese. Sprinkle with cinnamon sugar mixture. Roll up beginning at long end. Slice into ½-inch sections, place in an 8-inch cake pan that has been sprayed with nonstick cooking spray. Bake in a 375° oven for 10 minutes or until golden brown. Drizzle with glaze.

Glaze:

½	cup powdered sugar
¼	teaspoon vanilla
1	tablespoon milk

Combine all ingredients and stir until smooth.

Note: Finely chopped pecans sprinkled in add a nice touch to these delicious bite-size treats!

You never knew refrigerated crescent roll dough could taste sooo good!

To make this recipe even quicker, I keep a shaker filled with sugar and cinnamon on hand. To do this combine 1 cup of granulated sugar with 4 to 5 teaspoons of cinnamon. Keep it in a shaker container and you will have it ready for this recipe and breakfast favorites like cinnamon toast.

Note: To save time, soften cream cheese in the microwave. Place in a microwave safe bowl and heat at 50% power for 20 to 30 seconds.

Breakfast

*T*his special breakfast treat is one of our children's favorite meals. Yes, it takes a little more effort than using a boxed mix, but the results are worth it! Our children love waffles but we don't always have time to fix them for breakfast, so about once a month, we have breakfast for dinner. Okay, it may not be the most nutritious dinner but it provides a priceless opportunity to make family memories and besides, you are almost always guaranteed to make everybody happy!

Waffles

3	eggs, beaten
1	cup milk
1	stick of butter, melted
1	tablespoon vanilla
2	cups flour
½	teaspoon salt
1	tablespoon baking powder
2	teaspoons sugar

In a mixing bowl combine eggs, milk, melted butter, and vanilla; beat well. In another bowl combine dry ingredients. Gradually stir dry ingredients into egg mixture, and mix well. In a preheated waffle maker, cook until golden brown. Times vary, so cook according to your waffle maker's instructions. Serve with melted butter and warm syrup or top with fresh strawberries and whipped cream.

Yield: 6-8 waffles

Note: If you mix your batter in a batter bowl, or any bowl with a pouring spout, it will make it easier and neater to pour the batter into the waffle maker.

Hearty Pecan Pancakes

2	cups dry pancake mix
1	cup quick oats
¼	teaspoon salt
1	tablespoon cinnamon
1	tablespoon vanilla
2	cups club soda
½	cup finely chopped pecans

Place pancake mix, oats, salt, and cinnamon in a bowl. Add vanilla and club soda; mix well. Stir in pecans. Let sit 2 minutes so batter will thicken. Pour onto hot griddle to form large-size pancakes. Turn when pancakes bubble around the edges and are golden brown. Serve with melted butter and warm syrup.

Yield: 8 pancakes

Note: I use Aunt Jemima's Complete Pancake and Waffle Mix.

*Y*our family will enjoy these delicious pancakes. Our family loves them and so do our overnight guests! Be sure and take the time to warm the syrup. It taste so much better on the steaming hot pancakes. Remember, it is the little extras that make things special!

Note: The club soda makes the batter bubbly and thick. These pancakes may require a few extra minutes on your griddle.

Breakfast

A special Saturday morning treat! This recipe does require a little extra time but is well worth it.

Serving Suggestion: Top with sliced bananas or fresh strawberries for an extra special treat!

Texas-Style French Toast

1	small loaf Texas size white bread (thick slice)
3	cups light cream
12	eggs, well beaten
½	teaspoon salt
1	teaspoon cinnamon

Trim crust off 8 slices of bread; cut each slice into two triangles. Whip together cream, eggs, salt, and cinnamon. Dip triangles into egg mixture allowing each piece to absorb as much as possible. Place in ½-inch of hot vegetable oil (an electric skillet works well). Cook until golden brown turning only once. Put browned triangles in a shallow baking pan. Bake in a 400° oven for 3 to 5 minutes until puffy. Drain well on paper towels. To serve, sprinkle with confectioner's sugar and provide plenty of warm syrup.

Grammy's Rolls

2	packages yeast
2	cups lukewarm water
½	cup sugar
½	cup shortening
1	tablespoon salt
2	eggs
6	cups flour, unsifted

Dissolve yeast in water and set aside. With your mixer, cream sugar and shortening. Add eggs and salt. Alternately add yeast-water mixture and flour. (If you have dough hooks for your mixer, use them). Turn dough out onto a floured surface and knead until it gets stiff. Place dough in refrigerator for several hours or overnight. Make into rolls and let rise for 30 minutes to 1 hour. Bake in a preheated 325° oven for 15 to 20 minutes.

Yield: 24 rolls

Note: Mom says you do not have to refrigerate the dough. Let it rise in the bowl; punch down and then make into rolls. Let rolls rise again, then follow instructions for baking.

Note: These rolls freeze well. Mom often makes the rolls ahead of time and cooks them until they are just lightly browned. She then freezes them in the pan, thaws them at room temperature, and reheats the rolls before the meal.

My mom, known as "Grammy" to her grandkids, makes these wonderful rolls for every family holiday. The recipe was given to her by her mother Eunice Owen, and has been enjoyed for generations.

If (and that's a big if) you have rolls left over, they are great toasted for breakfast. Cut them in half, spread them with a little butter (or a lot) and toast them under the broiler of your oven until golden brown.

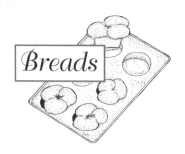

Breads

*S*our cream gives these little biscuits a wonderful taste and using biscuit mix makes them quick and easy to make!

*A*nother quick and easy bread. Making these rolls in a muffin tin gives them a nice round shape and makes a perfect addition to a luncheon salad plate or a plate of pasta!

Sour Cream Biscuits

½   cup butter, softened
1   (8-ounce) carton sour cream
2   cups biscuit mix

Cream butter, add sour cream and mix well. Gradually stir in biscuit mix until all ingredients are moistened. Spoon into greased mini-sized muffin tins; fill ⅔ full. Bake in a preheated 350° oven for 15 minutes.

Quick Parmesan Crescent Rolls

1 (8-ounce) can crescent rolls
butter or margarine
Parmesan cheese

Unroll the dough from a can of ready-to-bake crescent rolls. Separate into triangles and lightly butter each roll. Roll each triangle according to package directions. Place in a greased muffin tin (curve it to fit). Sprinkle lightly with parmesan cheese. Bake at 375° for 10 to 12 minutes or until golden brown.

Yield: 8 rolls

Susan's Cheese Rolls

2	sticks butter or margarine
½	cup sugar
½	teaspoon salt
4	cups all-purpose flour
1	cup cold milk
2	teaspoons dry yeast
2	eggs, beaten
2	cups grated Cheddar cheese

In a saucepan over low heat, melt butter, sugar, and salt. Remove from heat, add cold milk and stir in yeast. Now add the eggs and gradually stir in flour until well mixed. The dough will be gooey. Place in a covered dish and refrigerate overnight. Take out and place on a flour coated work area and let rest for 15 minutes. Coat your hands with flour; pinch off a small amount of dough (enough to make a ball the size of a small walnut); flatten the piece and place a small amount of grated cheese in the center. Fold the dough around the cheese and roll into a ball. Place three balls in each cup of a muffin pan that has been sprayed with nonstick cooking spray. Repeat with remaining dough. Let rolls rise about 30 minutes. Bake in a preheated 400° oven for 7 to 10 minutes or until golden brown.

Yield: 18 rolls

I love to make these rolls! My family says they melt in your mouth. I also like the fact that the rolls are so easy to make. Simply make the dough the night before, let rise overnight in the refrigerator, then make your rolls out the next day. You can bake the rolls ahead of time and freeze them, but they are best right out of the oven.

Note: Don't be afraid to try making yeast rolls. This is an easy recipe to start with. Plus the compliments you receive on these rolls will be all the encouragement you need!

41

Breads

I've had this recipe since high school. Batter bread was a popular bread served in our school cafeteria. My family teased me about this recipe until they tasted it. Now they often ask for "school bread".

Serving Suggestion: The flavor of this bread is especially good with barbeque!

Note: This bread does not reheat well. That is usually not a problem because there are rarely any leftovers!

Batter Bread

1	package yeast
¾	cup warm water
2	cups flour
½	cup oatmeal
½	teaspoon salt
½	cup dry milk
¼	cup sugar
1	egg
¼	cup melted butter

Preheat oven to 375°. In a small bowl or 2-cup glass measuring cup, empty 1 package of yeast into ¾ cup of warm water. Let sit 3 to 4 minutes. In a large bowl, mix the flour, oatmeal, and salt. To the yeast mixture, add the dry milk and sugar; stir well. Stir in the egg. Slowly add liquid mixture to dry ingredients and mix well. Add melted butter and stir. Spread dough evenly in a shallow greased 9x9-inch pan. Let rise in a warm, draft-free area until double in bulk. Put small pats of butter on top. Bake 15 to 20 minutes or until bread is golden brown on top. Serve warm!

Breads

Dell's Cornbread Muffins

1	cup all-purpose flour
1	cup yellow cornmeal
4	teaspoons baking powder
1	tablespoon sugar
2	teaspoons salt
2	eggs, beaten
1½	cups milk
¼	cup butter, melted
⅛	cup diced red pepper
⅛	cup diced green pepper
1	cup grated cheddar cheese

Prepare cast iron muffin or cornbread stick pan by spraying lightly with nonstick cooking spray. Preheat oven to 375°. Place cast iron pan in the preheated oven to get hot. Combine all dry ingredients in a large bowl. In a small bowl mix eggs, milk, and melted butter. Add egg mixture to dry ingredients then stir in peppers and cheese; mix well. Pour into hot muffin pans (fill ⅔ full) and bake for 15 to 20 minutes or until brown.

*I*f you prefer plain cornbread, just omit the peppers and cheese, or spice it up with some diced jalapeno and whole kernel corn. Any way you make it, this is a great cornbread recipe!

Serving Suggestion: Great served with a bowl of homemade Beef Stew (page 63) or Texas Chili (page 60).

43

Breads

*classic
southern bread, my
Granny, Eunice Owen,
served cornbread at
every meal. It tasted
so good with the fresh
corn and peas from her
garden or split open
and covered with
vegetable soup!*

*aydiene loved
cornbread. Her favorite
variation was always
the ones with a
Tex-Mex flavor like this
one filled with cheese
and green chilies. It has
just the right spice to it!*

Mom's Cornbread

2	cups cornmeal
1	cup flour
1	tablespoon baking powder
1	teaspoon salt
2	tablespoons sugar
1½	cups milk
2	tablespoons butter, melted
2	eggs, beaten

Combine all ingredients and mix well. Pour into hot greased cast iron muffin pans. Bake in a 425° oven for 15 to 20 minutes or until golden brown.

New Mexico Spoon Bread

1½	cups cornmeal
½	teaspoon baking soda
1	teaspoon baking powder
1	teaspoon salt
1	teaspoon sugar
⅓	cup melted shortening
1	(15-ounce) can cream style corn
2	eggs, slightly beaten
2	(4-ounce) cans green chilies
1½	cups grated cheddar cheese

Mix all ingredients except chilies and cheese. Pour half the batter into a greased 9x9 inch pan. Layer half the chilies and half the cheese over batter. Add remaining batter and top with remaining chilies and cheese. Bake in 400° oven for 30 minutes or until lightly brown on top.

Jalapeno Cornbread

3	cups cornbread mix
3	eggs, beaten
2	tablespoons sugar
½	cup vegetable oil
1	(15-ounce) can cream-style corn
1	(3-ounce) can jalapenos, seeded and finely chopped
½	onion, chopped
1½	cups milk
1½	cups grated cheddar cheese

Combine all ingredients and stir well. Pour into a well greased 10x13-inch pan. Bake at 350° for 30 to 45 minutes.

Cornbread is a southern staple. In Texas, we spice it up with jalapenos!

Cornbread Especial

1	(8½-ounce) package cornbread mix
1	cup fried onions
1	(8-ounce) carton sour cream
1	cup grated cheddar cheese
1	teaspoon salt

Prepare cornbread according to package directions. Pour into a well greased 9x9-inch pan. Sprinkle fried onion rings on top. Combine sour cream and grated cheddar cheese, add salt and stir well. Spoon cheese mixture on top. Spread with knife and marble into cornbread mixture a little. Bake at 375° for 20 to 30 minutes or until golden brown.

You will love this unique cornbread. It has a great flavor and is so easy to make!

Serving Suggestion: Great with chili! For a quick meal cut cornbread into squares and spoon chili on top.

45

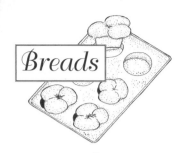

Breads

*N*aydiene simply called this cornbread Mexican Cornbread not telling her guests that it included broccoli. She knew they would like it if they would just taste it. She was right!

A recipe from my days as a Girl Scout. We had this bread on campouts as a special treat. It is similar to sopapillas. Yummy!

To make Cinnamon Butter combine:
1 stick butter (softened) with 4 teaspoons brown sugar and 1 teaspoon cinnamon in a small bowl. Beat ingredients until fluffy. Chill.

Broccoli Cornbread

1	(8-ounce) package Mexican cornbread mix
½	cup margarine, melted
⅓	cup diced onion
1	teaspoon salt
¾	cup cottage cheese
1	(10-ounce) package frozen chopped broccoli, thawed and drained
4	eggs, slightly beaten

Combine all ingredients. Pour into a greased 9x13 inch pan. Bake at 400° for 30 minutes.

Camp Bread

1	package dry yeast
1½	cups warm water
1	teaspoon salt
6	tablespoons shortening
¼	cup sugar
3 to 4	cups flour

Dissolve yeast in warm water; set aside for 3 minutes. Combine remaining ingredients in a large bowl. Add yeast and mix well. Let stand for 30 minutes. Pinch off pieces and flatten out with hand into approximately 3-inch squares. Fry in vegetable oil until golden brown. Drain on paper towels; then roll in powdered sugar. Serve warm with honey and cinnamon butter.

Quick Bread Sticks

1   package of hot dog buns
1   stick of butter, melted
garlic powder to taste
onion powder to taste
seasoned salt to taste

With a sharp knife, cut buns (tops and bottoms) lengthwise in half to make four sticks. Separate into sticks and place face up on an ungreased cookie sheet. Lightly brush buns with melted butter, then sprinkle lightly with the next three ingredients. Bake in a 250° oven for 30 to 45 minutes. Bread should be dry and crisp. May be stored for several days in an airtight container or plastic bag.

Parmesan Sticks

1   package of hot dog buns
1   stick butter, melted
Parmesan cheese
seasoned salt to taste
sesame seeds

Slice hot dog buns lengthwise to make four bread sticks. Dip in melted butter and sprinkle with Parmesan cheese, seasoned salt, and sesame seeds. Brown in a 250° oven for 30 to 45 minutes until crisp.

Who would have thought that hot dog buns could taste so good?! These easy to make bread sticks are delicious!

Serving Suggestion: Cut or break bread sticks into cubes to make great seasoned croutons for your salads.

Another quick and easy bread. Great served with your favorite pasta or salad.

Breads

*T*his is one of Dell's favorite breads for breakfast. He loves to toast several slices of this wonderful bread under the broiler and eat it hot with lots of butter!

Serving Suggestion: This bread makes a delicious party sandwich for a shower or tea. Slice very thin and spread with cream cheese that has been flavored with honey and lemon.

Spiced Apricot Bread

1½	cups dried apricots, diced
1	cup sugar
½	teaspoon cloves
¼	teaspoon nutmeg
½	teaspoon cinnamon
½	teaspoon salt
2	tablespoons butter
1	cup water
1	egg, beaten
2	cups flour
1	teaspoon baking soda
1	cup walnuts or pecans, chopped

Combine apricots, sugar, spices, butter, and water in saucepan. Cook 5 minutes; cool thoroughly. Add beaten egg. Stir soda into flour and add to apricot mixture. Add nuts and stir until blended. Pour into a greased loaf pan or mini loaf pans. Bake large loaf for 1 hour at 350°. Remove from pan, let cool. Chill overnight.

Breads

Pumpkin Pecan Bread

3½	cups flour
2	teaspoons baking soda
1	teaspoon salt
1½	teaspoons cinnamon
1	teaspoon nutmeg
1	cup sugar
1	cup vegetable oil
4	eggs
⅔	cup water
2	cups canned pumpkin
1	cup chopped pecans

*S*hare a loaf with your children's teachers or your co-workers during the holidays.

Combine flour, soda, salt, cinnamon, and nutmeg in a large bowl. Add sugar and stir until thoroughly mixed. Combine oil, eggs, water, and pumpkin in another bowl. Make a well in the center of the flour mixture; pour in pumpkin mixture. Stir until well blended; add nuts. Pour into four 4x8-inch, greased loaf pans filling each ½ full. Bake at 350˚ for 50 to 60 minutes or until toothpick comes out clean.

Yield: 4 loaves

Note: Coat pecans lightly with flour. This will keep them from sinking to the bottom of the bread.

Serving Suggestion: Bake in shaped bread pans. Then slice thin and fill with cream cheese for party sandwiches. Great for fall coffees or teas!

49

Breads

Always a favorite! This bread is so easy to make and a perfect way to use those ripe bananas.

Good any way you slice it... warm out of the oven, chilled, or toasted for breakfast!

Banana Nut Bread

2	cups flour
1	teaspoon baking powder
½	teaspoon soda
1	teaspoon salt
1	stick margarine
1	cup sugar
2	eggs
1	cup mashed bananas
¾	cup chopped pecans (coat with 1 tablespoon of flour)

Sift together dry ingredients; set aside. Cream margarine and sugar together until creamy. Add eggs and mashed bananas; blend well. Pour in dry ingredients; mix well. Stir in chopped nuts. Pour into greased loaf pan and bake at 350° for 50 minutes to 1 hour.

Yield: 1 loaf

Note: Coating the pecans with flour keeps them from sinking to the bottom of the bread.

It will take at least 2 bananas to get 1 cup of mashed bananas.

Also, if bread begins to brown too quickly on top, tent with foil.

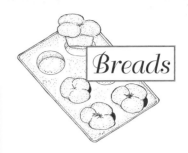

Cherry Pecan Bread

¾	cup sugar
½	cup butter
2	eggs
2½	cups sifted all-purpose flour
1	teaspoon baking soda
½	teaspoon salt
1	cup buttermilk
1	cup chopped pecans
1	(10-ounce) jar Maraschino cherries, drained, and finely chopped
1	teaspoon vanilla

Cream sugar and butter together. Add eggs then beat until light and fluffy. Sift together flour, baking soda, and salt. Alternately add the dry ingredients and buttermilk to creamed mixture. Mix until well blended. Gently stir in nuts, cherries, and vanilla. Pour into a greased loaf pan. Bake at 350° for 55 to 60 minutes; remove from pan and cool.

Note: Halfway through the baking process loosely cover with foil to keep the top from getting too brown. Remove foil for the last 10 to 15 minutes.

Another great holiday bread! Bake in mini loaf pans for gift giving. This bread is also good toasted for breakfast!

Helpful Hint: Coating the pecans lightly with flour keeps them from sinking to the bottom of the bread. They will be more evenly distributed throughout the bread when coated with 1 tablespoon of flour.

Bread Machine Pizza Dough

(for a 1½ pound bread machine)

*T*his dough is also great for making calzones. Separate dough into four equal pieces. Press the dough out into 6-inch circles. Spread pizza sauce over one half of the circle. Cover sauce with your favorite pizza toppings, including mozzarella cheese. Fold dough over and seal edges (brush edges with water before sealing). Bake in a preheated 450° oven for 15 to 20 minutes or until golden brown.

3	cups all-purpose flour
1	teaspoon salt
2	teaspoons active dry yeast
1	tablespoon sugar
2	tablespoons olive oil
1	cup warm water (for Welbilt or Dak machines add 2 additional tablespoons)

Place all ingredients in the bread machine, select the dough setting and press start. If time allows, let machine complete the full kneading and rising cycle. If pressed for time, stop the machine after it has finished the first kneading cycle (the crust will rise when cooked). Transfer to an 18-inch pizza pan that has been sprayed with nonstick cooking spray. Gently stretch dough to fit pan and then pinch dough around edges to form a lip. Spread dough with your favorite pizza sauce and add your toppings of choice. Bake in a preheated 450° oven for 15 to 20 minutes or until crust is lightly browned.

Note: Spray your hands with nonstick cooking spray and dough will be easier to handle as you stretch it to fit the pizza pan.

Mrs. Shepherd's
Whole Wheat Bread

3	packages yeast (dissolve in ⅓ cup warm water)
1½	cups scalded milk
1½	cups hot water (not boiling, hot tap water is fine)
2	tablespoons black strap molasses
4	tablespoons vegetable oil
½	cup brown sugar (may add more is desired)
⅓-½	cup wheat germ
3½	teaspoons salt
⅓-½	cup cornmeal
4	cups stone-ground wheat flour, divided
4	cups white flour, divided

Dissolve yeast in warm water. Scald milk, cool to lukewarm. In a large bowl (do not use a metal bowl), add water, molasses, oil and brown sugar. Add 2 cups of wheat flour then add yeast. Add wheat germ, salt, cornmeal, 2 cups of wheat flour, and 3 cups of white flour. Work in the last cup of white flour while kneading. Knead dough for approximately 10 minutes. Grease a large bowl, place it in the oven at a low temperature for just a few minutes until bowl is warm. Place dough in bowl. Set in a draft free place and let rise until double in size. Punch down and let rise again. Grease 4 bread pans. Shape dough into loaves and place in pans. Let rise 15 minutes. Bake at 350° for 10 minutes. Cover with foil, turn oven temperature down to 325° and cook an additional 20 minutes or until brown on top.

*M*rs. Shepherd was a dear family friend. Her husband, M. L. Shepherd, and my grandfather, Durward West, were in the Navy together in World War I. I was fortunate to live next door to her while I attended Texas Tech University. She was kind enough to share this recipe. It is a wonderful hearty bread that does take some time and patience. But you know, we all might find it therapeutic to slow down for awhile and make bread from scratch. Plus the smell of bread baking always makes us feel better!

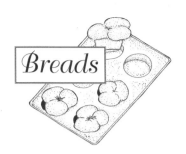

Breads

Our daughter Kaitlyn loves to make pretzels, however, very few of them end up looking like traditional pretzels. Instead, they take the shape of letters, numbers, or funny looking animals. This recipe is delicious and makes a great first time cooking project. Have fun!

Kaitlyn's Favorite Pretzels

½	cup warm water
1	package (or 2 teaspoons) dry yeast
1	large egg, separated
¼	cup sugar
⅓	cup butter
¾	cup milk
½	teaspoon salt
4½	cups all purpose flour
1	tablespoon water
¼	cup pretzel salt or other coarse salt

Combine yeast and warm water; set aside for 5 minutes. Mix together egg yolk, sugar, butter, and milk; add yeast and blend well. Combine salt and flour. Add enough flour to egg-yeast mixture to make a stiff dough. Sprinkle a clean work surface with flour. Knead the dough until smooth and elastic (about 5 minutes). Let the dough rise for one hour. Pull the dough into equal pieces. Roll each piece into a rope and shape. Dough can be shaped into the traditional pretzel shape or whatever shape you desire (letters, numbers etc.). Carefully move pretzels on to greased baking sheets. Add tablespoon of water to egg white; brush on pretzel and sprinkle with coarse salt. Bake at 425° for 15 to 20 minutes.

Variation:
Brush uncooked pretzel with egg white but omit the pretzel salt. Bake according to directions. Immediately after removing from the oven brush with melted butter and roll in a mixture of cinnamon and sugar. Serve warm.

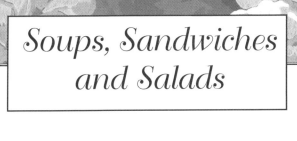

Soups, Sandwiches and Salads

*Happiness,
like good
soup,
is always
homemade.*

Lessons from the Dinner Table

Our busy lives have driven us out of the kitchen, into the fast-food lane of drive-through meals, and eating in the car! Sadly, we have lost the time spent around the family dinner table. We rationalize it by saying, "This is not the 1950's anymore," but we all ache for a slower pace and a time to rest.

The dinner table is not just a place to eat. It is a place where many life lessons are taught. In fact, you can learn a lot from a bowl of mashed potatoes. For example, you learn patience as you wait for the steaming bowl to be passed around. You learn moderation as your mother cautions you not to take too big a spoonful, and you learn to think of others because you don't take all of the last serving.

When we give up eating together around the dinner table we also give up the opportunity to teach our children table manners and the art of conversation. Most importantly, we take away the opportunity for our children to be heard, to have a safe forum away from the world, a place where they can express their dreams and not be laughed at. All children yearn for this. They need a time to refresh themselves so they can go out and battle the world and strive to make their dreams come true!

Cheesy Chicken Vegetable Soup

4	boneless, skinless chicken breasts
8	cups water
2	teaspoons salt
1	teaspoon pepper
¾	cup chopped onion
1	cup diced celery
1½	cups diced carrots
2	cups diced potatoes
3	cups cooked rice
4	chicken bouillon cubes
1	(1-pound) package mild Mexican Velveeta cheese, cubed

A very hearty soup that will satisfy your hunger and warm your soul on a cold winter night! Our family loves this soup. Just add salad and bread for a complete meal.

Bring water, salt, pepper, and chicken to a boil; reduce heat and simmer 30 minutes or until chicken is done. Remove chicken, reserving broth. Chop chicken into bite-size pieces and return to broth. Add onion, celery, carrots, potatoes, cooked rice, and bouillon cubes. Bring to a boil; reduce heat and simmer for 45 minutes, stirring occasionally. Add cheese, stir, and heat until cheese melts.

Note: The rice must be cooked before it is added, otherwise it will settle into clumps at the bottom of the pot. (I speak from experience!) I prefer to use Uncle Ben's Converted Rice.

Note: For an even thicker soup, add another package of cheese.

Naydiene's Cheese Broccoli Soup

*N*aydiene often made this soup and took it to her friends that were also widows or shut-ins. I can't think of anything nicer than a hot bowl of soup and the warmth of friendship to make someone feel better. We often enjoy this soup after a busy day. It is quick and easy to make.

Serving Suggestion: Serve with Quick Bread Sticks (page 47).

1	(10 ¾- ounce) can cream of celery soup
1	(10 ¾-ounce) can Cheddar cheese soup
1	soup can of milk
¼	teaspoon garlic powder
¼	teaspoon onion powder
dash	black pepper
2	cups grated Cheddar cheese
3	cups chopped broccoli, cooked

In a saucepan, combine soups, milk, garlic powder,onion powder, and pepper. Stir mixture occasionally over low heat until hot. Add grated cheese. Stir until cheese melts. Add 2 to 3 cups of cooked chopped broccoli. Stir and continue cooking over low heat until soup is hot. Serve immediately.

Note: While you are heating the soups and waiting for the cheese to melt, you can prepare broccoli spears in your microwave. By using spears and chopping it yourself, you end up with higher quality broccoli than found in most prepackaged chopped broccoli.

Susan's Taco Soup

2	pounds ground beef
1	small onion, chopped
1	(7-ounce) can of chopped green chilies
1	teaspoon salt
½	teaspoon pepper
1	package taco seasoning mix
1	package dry ranch dressing mix
1	(11-ounce) can of corn
1	(23-ounce) can Ranch Style beans
1	(10-ounce) can diced tomatoes with chilies
1	cup water or as needed

I love this soup! First, because it is so easy and second, because it tastes great.

Note: This soup makes a lot and freezes well.

Brown meat and onion. Drain. Add remaining ingredients. Bring to a boil then reduce heat. Simmer for 30 minutes. Serve this soup topped with grated Cheddar cheese.

Serves: 6 to 8

*C*hili is a Texas favorite and nothing beats a bowl of chili served with tortillas on a cold winter day!

Note: The Jardiene's chili seasoning package contains a packet of mesa flour. I normally leave it out; especially when serving with tortillas or serving the chili over tamales.

Serving Suggestion: This is also great served over corn chips and topped with grated Cheddar cheese!

Texas Chili

2	pounds round steak or other lean cut of beef
1	tablespoon oil
1	package of D.L. Jardiene's Chili Seasoning mix
1	(28-ounce) can diced tomatoes with juice
	salt to taste

Trim fat off of meat and grind. Brown meat in oil. Drain well. Add Jardiene's Chili Seasoning Mix. Set mesa flour packet aside. I normally add ¼ teaspoon of the red pepper for a mild spicy flavor. (You can adjust according to your taste, but I find this pleases most.) Where instructions call for tomato sauce, substitute a 28-ounce can of diced tomatoes including juice. Add water as needed. Simmer for 1 to 2 hours or until meat is tender. Note: Real Texas chili does not have beans! Serve chili topped with grated Cheddar cheese and warm tortillas on the side.

Yield: 6 servings

Note: Your chili will be leaner and more flavorful if you trim and grind your own meat. I use my food processor to coarsely grind inexpensive cuts like arm roast or any other cut that might be on sale instead of using prepackaged chili meat that is full of fat and gristle.

Note: Jardiene's Chili Seasoning Mix is available at gourmet food and specialty stores.

Quick Tortilla Soup

3	boneless, skinless chicken breasts
6	cups of water
½	onion, chopped
1	medium green pepper, chopped
½	cup diced celery
2	tablespoons butter
1	cup frozen whole kernel corn
2	(10-ounce) cans chopped tomatoes with chilies
1	package taco seasoning
1	package dry ranch dressing mix

salt and pepper to taste
white corn tortilla chips
grated Cheddar cheese
chopped green onion

Another quick and easy favorite to serve on a cold winter day. A simmering pot of this soup fills your kitchen with a wonderful aroma!

Note: I do not see any reason to spend time frying tortilla strips for this soup like many recipes suggest. I have found that the white corn tortilla chips work just as well.

Cook chicken in water until done (approximately 30 minutes). Remove chicken, cut into bite-size pieces, and return to chicken broth. Saute onion, green pepper, and celery in butter until tender. Add to chicken and broth. Add corn, tomatoes with chilies, taco seasoning, and ranch dressing mix. Simmer 30 to 40 minutes. Place tortilla chips in bowls. Ladle soup over chips and top with grated Cheddar cheese and diced green onions. Serve immediately.

Yield: 6 servings

Green Chile Beef Stew

A Texas twist to regular beef stew, this stew is full of flavor and has a little kick to it. The green chilies keep it mild enough though so the whole family can enjoy it.

2	tablespoons olive oil
1	medium onion, chopped
1	clove garlic, minced
2	pounds lean stew meat
6	cups water
½	teaspoon fresh ground pepper
½	teaspoon cumin
4	teaspoons salt, divided
1	(7-ounce) can green chilies, divided
3-4	medium potatoes, cut into 1- inch chunks

Sauté garlic and onion in olive oil until transparent. Add meat, browning on all sides. Add water, pepper, cumin, 2 teaspoons of salt, and ½ can of green chilies. Simmer for 2 hours. Add potatoes, remaining salt and green chilies. Turn heat to medium and cook with lid off for an additional 30 minutes or until potatoes are completely done. Potatoes should be somewhat mushy so as to thicken the stew.

Yield: 6 servings

Beef Stew

2	tablespoons oil
2	pounds beef stew meat
1	medium onion, chopped
1	clove garlic
4	cups boiling water
1	(15-ounce) can tomato sauce
1	tablespoon salt
1	tablespoon lemon juice
1	teaspoon sugar
1	tablespoon Worcestershire sauce
½	teaspoon pepper
½	teaspoon paprika
4	carrots, cut in bite-size pieces
3	potatoes, cut in chunks
2	stalks of celery, chopped

Brown meat in oil. Add onion and the next 9 ingredients. Cover and simmer for 1½ to 2 hours or until meat is tender. Stir occasionally. Remove garlic. Add carrots, potatoes, and celery. Cook another 15 to 20 minutes or until potatoes and carrots are tender.

Yield: 6 servings

A classic family favorite! Add cornbread and a salad for a great meal.

Note: To save money I purchase a family size package of thick round steak or whatever is on special and cut my own stew meat. This does take a little extra time but I find that it is worth the effort because you get better quality meat and more for your money!

*P*ork tenderloin is always a treat, but when marinated with this combination of flavors, it is extra special!

Serve with:

Roasted Garlic Mayonnaise

2 cups mayonnaise
1 tablespoon chopped roasted garlic
¼ teaspoon seasoned salt
¼ teaspoon freshly ground black pepper

Combine ingredients, mixing thoroughly. Refrigerate for 8 hours before serving.

Marinated Pork Sandwiches

3	(¾-pound) pork tenderloins
½	cup roasted garlic infused olive oil
3	tablespoons grated onion
3	tablespoons white wine vinegar
½	teaspoon chili powder
¾	teaspoon garlic powder
½	teaspoon dried oregano
½	teaspoon cumin
¾	teaspoon coarsely ground black pepper
½	teaspoon salt
2	tablespoons melted butter

Place tenderloins in large zip-top plastic bag. Combine oil, onion, vinegar and seasonings. Add marinade to bag, seal and shake to thoroughly coat meat. Place bag in refrigerator and allow meat to marinate for 8 hours, occasionally turning bag. Remove tenderloins from bag and reserve marinade. Combine reserved marinade with melted butter and baste tenderloins occasionally while cooking. Place tenderloins on the rack of a shallow roasting pan. Bake in a 425° oven for 10 minutes. Reduce heat to 350° and bake an additional 25 to 30 minutes or until meat thermometer reads 160°. Cut into ¼-inch slices and serve with roasted garlic mayonnaise and small sandwich rolls.

Rye Bread Party Pizzas

1	pound ground beef
1	pound mild or hot sausage
1	pound processed cheese loaf
1	tablespoon Worcestershire sauce
1	teaspoon oregano
½	teaspoon garlic powder
½	teaspoon salt
¼	teaspoon pepper
2	loaves party rye bread

Brown ground beef and sausage together, drain well. Add cheese; heat until cheese melts. Add next 5 ingredients. Stir well. Spread on rye bread. Place on a cookie sheet and heat in a 350° oven until bubbly and lightly toasted. Serve warm as an appetizer or as a tasty treat with soup.

Note: This recipe makes a lot so you can prepare 1 loaf and freeze the rest.

Most often this is served as an appetizer, but we find the hearty flavor makes a perfect sandwich to serve with a bowl of soup or a salad. Plus, they are so easy to prepare!

Note: These freeze well.

65

favorite with our entire family, this sandwich can be made with refrigerated bread dough available at your local grocer. If you have a bread machine use our pizza dough recipe, it makes this sandwich delicious!

Stromboli "Pizza Sandwich"

Prepare pizza dough in bread machine (page 52) or purchase refrigerated dough.

Filling:

½	pound ground beef
½	cup chopped onion
2	tablespoons prepared mustard
8	slices American cheese
2	cups grated Mozzarella or prepackaged pizza cheese
½	cup Parmesan cheese
1	(4-ounce) package sliced pepperoni
1	(8-ounce) package sliced Canadian bacon, chopped
1	teaspoon olive oil

Brown ground beef and onion until meat is cooked and onion is tender. Drain well. Set aside. Spread pizza dough out on lightly floured surface and shape into a 12x12-inch rectangle. Spread dough with mustard, leaving a ½-inch border of dough around the edges. Layer 4 slices of American cheese lengthwise down center of dough. Sprinkle ground beef over cheese slices. Layer on pepperoni and Canadian bacon. Sprinkle with cheeses leaving border at top and bottom of dough. Top with additional slices of American Cheese. Wet edges of dough and fold sides over filling. Seal by pinching seam in middle and on ends. Transfer to greased baking sheet and brush with oil. Bake at 350° for 20 minutes or until lightly browned. Let set for 5 minutes. Slice with a serrated knife. Serve warm.

Favorite Tuna Sandwich

2	(6-ounce) cans Albacore tuna in spring water, drained
¼	cup diced celery
4	teaspoons sweet relish
5	tablespoons Hellman's mayonnaise
¾	teaspoon onion powder
2	teaspoons dried chives
⅛	teaspoon curry powder
¼	cup chopped pecans
	salt and pepper to taste

Mix above ingredients together until well blended. Serve on whole wheat bread with lettuce.

*Note: Many people do not think they like tuna because they have only eaten less expensive dark meat tuna packed in oil. There is **no substitute** for Albacore tuna! It is a little more expensive but worth it.*

The best tuna sandwich you have ever tasted and one of my husband's favorites!

Note: If you prefer you can leave the curry powder out. But don't be afraid to try it, the curry gives the tuna sandwich a nice flavor.

*A*nother favorite!
This sandwich has a
wonderful flavor and is
a nice change of pace
from a cold ham and
cheese!

Note: You can
prepare the filling
ahead of time and
refrigerate until you
are ready to assemble
the sandwiches.

Hot Chicken Salad Sandwiches

3	cups cooked chicken, chopped
1	hard boiled egg, chopped
2	tablespoons chopped green pepper
2	tablespoons diced onion
1	tablespoon sweet pickle relish
3	tablespoons stuffed green olives, chopped
1	cup grated Cheddar cheese
½	cup mayonnaise
1	teaspoon lemon juice
salt and pepper to taste	
4	french rolls cut in half, lengthwise

Combine all ingredients except rolls and mix well. Fill rolls and wrap each sandwich in foil. Bake in a 300° oven for 20 minutes or until cheese is melted and filling is hot. Remove from foil and serve immediately.

Yield: 4 sandwiches

Savory Chicken Salad

4 to 5	cups cooked chicken breasts, cut into bite-size pieces
1	stick butter, melted
2	cups Hellman's mayonnaise
½	teaspoon curry powder
¼	teaspoon garlic powder
2	cups seedless red grapes, cut in half
½	cup toasted sliced almonds

salt and pepper to taste

Cook chicken breasts in boiling water until done. While chicken is cooking, melt butter in microwave. Set aside and let cool until it is room temperature. Chop cooked chicken into bite-size pieces; sprinkle with salt and pepper to taste. Toast almonds. In a bowl, combine butter and mayonnaise with a whisk until creamy. Add curry and garlic powder; stir until well blended. Gently stir in chicken, grapes, and toasted almonds. Refrigerate until well chilled. Serve on a lettuce leaf.

Yield: 4-6 servings

Note: I prefer to use boneless, skinless chicken breasts. Five large breasts should give you enough chicken for 4 cups.

The best chicken salad I have ever tasted! It has just the right touch of curry and the sweet red grapes give it color and flavor. It is always a big hit when served and a most requested recipe!

Note: Toast almonds in your oven at 350°, stirring occasionally, for 10 to 12 minutes.

*A*n all-time family favorite and another one of our most requested recipes.

Don't leave out the cayenne pepper, it adds just the right "zip"! Be sure and measure carefully, a little goes a long way. One year we doubled the recipe to take to a family reunion. Somehow, Dell mis-measured and put in a little too much cayenne. Everyone loved the potato salad but were very careful not to get to far away from something to drink. Several commented that it had "quite a kick," and it did!

Dell's Creamy Potato Salad

6	cups red new potatoes with skins, cut into chunks
1	tablespoon salt, added to boiling water
1	cup sour cream
1	cup Hellman's mayonnaise
4	ribs celery, diced
6	green onions, tops and bottoms, diced
¼	cup diced pimentos, drained well
1½	teaspoons salt
½	teaspoon cayenne pepper

Wash potatoes well, trim off any bad spots. Cut into bite-size chunks. Place in large saucepan, add 1 tablespoon salt and water to cover. Boil until tender, being careful not to overcook. Drain well. In a large bowl, combine sour cream, mayonnaise, salt, and cayenne pepper; blend well. Stir in celery, green onions, and pimento. Gently stir in cooked potatoes until completely covered with dressing. Refrigerate until well chilled.

Yield: 8-10 servings

Note: If you are making this the day before it will be served, leave the onions out until an hour or two before it will be served. Otherwise, the onions tend to overpower the salad.

Marinated Vegetable Salad

1	(16-ounce) can tiny green peas
1	(11-ounce) can whole kernel corn
1	(16-ounce) can French-style green beans
½	onion, chopped
¾	cup diced celery
1	(2-ounce) jar diced pimento

A great make-ahead salad that will keep in the refrigerator for up to a week. It actually improves with age!

Drain all vegetables well. Pour into a large air-tight bowl.

Marinade:

½	cup light vegetable oil
½	cup wine vinegar
¾	cup sugar
1	teaspoon salt
½	teaspoon pepper

Combine ingredients in a saucepan. Bring to a boil, stirring occasionally. Boil for 1 minute, stirring to make sure sugar dissolves. Pour hot marinade over vegetables, cover and refrigerate for at least 12 hours.

Yield: 8 to 10 servings

Serving Suggestion: This salad goes well with Honey Glazed Ham (page119) and Dell's Creamy Potato Salad (page 70). It is also delicious with a sandwich and is a great way to get your family to eat their veggies!

Salads

favorite with our family, this classic slaw is great with barbeque, fried chicken, or as a side dish to any meal!

Note: For really crisp slaw, shred cabbage into a bowl and cover with ice water for one hour. Drain well, blot with paper towels, then refrigerate in zip-top plastic bags until ready to use.

Country-Style Creamy Coleslaw

½	large green cabbage, coarsely chopped
½	small purple cabbage, coarsely chopped
1½	cups shredded carrots
½	cup diced green pepper
¾	cup mayonnaise
¼	cup sour cream
3½	tablespoons sugar
5	tablespoons wine vinegar
1	teaspoon salt
½	teaspoon celery seed

Combine cabbage, carrots, and green pepper in a large bowl; set aside. Combine mayonnaise, sour cream, sugar, vinegar, and salt. Whisk until well combined and creamy. Stir in celery seed. Pour dressing over cabbage mixture, and toss well. Chill.

Yield: 8 servings

Copper Pennies

2	pounds carrots, peeled and sliced into rounds
1	onion, thinly sliced
1	green pepper, thinly sliced

Dressing:

1	(10 ¾-ounce) can tomato soup, undiluted
1	cup sugar
½	cup vinegar
1	tablespoon Worcestershire sauce
1	teaspoon prepared mustard
¾	cup vegetable oil
	salt and pepper to taste

*O*ften served at family reunions and summer picnics, this has been a family favorite for generations. It is another great make-ahead salad that improves in flavor if made a day before serving.

Cook carrots in salted water, just until tender; drain. Add onion and green pepper. Combine dressing ingredients and mix well. Pour over vegetables. Refrigerate overnight. Will keep in refrigerator for several days.

Yield: 12 to 16 servings

Hint: To save time I like to buy baby carrots that have already been peeled.

73

Salads

Our favorite green salad because it combines so many wonderful flavors and is such a pretty salad to serve.

Helpful Hint: To save time purchase a prepackaged assortment of European greens at your local grocer. This also gives the salad a gourmet look.

Slice and add avocados just before serving since they turn brown so quickly.

Note: This dressing has a tendency to separate, so be sure and shake well before pouring over the salad.

Napa Garden Salad

1	head, red-leaf lettuce
1	(11-ounce) can Mandarin oranges, well drained
1	small red onion, thinly sliced and separated into rings
1	avocado, sliced
1	cup red seedless grapes, cut in half

Wash and drain lettuce. (Lettuce will be crisper if you do this the day before and store in the refrigerator in a zip-top plastic bag.) Tear lettuce into bite size pieces. Place in a large salad bowl add remaining ingredients and toss. Serve with the following salad dressing.

Note: Your onion rings will be much crisper and sweeter if you place them in a bowl of ice water for 15 or 20 minutes. When ready to use, drain on paper towels and add to salad.

Dressing:

1	cup salad oil
⅓	cup vinegar
2	tablespoons sugar
2	teaspoons ketchup
2	teaspoons chili sauce
2	teaspoons prepared mustard
1	teaspoon salt

Combine all ingredients and whisk until well blended. This dressing is best if made the day before.

Mom's Pea Salad

2	(8.5-ounce) cans very young, small, sweet peas, chilled
½	cup sliced celery
⅓	cup sliced stuffed olives
½	cup cubed Cheddar cheese
2	cups shredded iceberg lettuce
⅛	teaspoon seasoned salt
⅛	teaspoon black pepper
2	teaspoons mayonnaise

Chill peas by placing cans in refrigerator a day or two before using. Drain peas *well*. In a bowl, combine peas, celery, olives, and lettuce. Season with seasoned salt and pepper. Gently stir in mayonnaise. Chill before serving.

Note: Unlike other pea salads, this pea salad requires very little mayonnaise. You use just enough to bind it together. It can be made ahead of time but do not add lettuce until just before serving, otherwise, the lettuce will become soggy. Be sure your lettuce is crisp and cold. Wash it a day ahead of time. Store in the refrigerator wrapped in a paper towel in a zip-top plastic bag.

Naydiene often served this salad. It was her own version, and as always she could improve something as simple as pea salad! This salad is lighter and more flavorful because it is not drowning in mayonnaise!

Salads

nother Naydiene specialty, this is one of our favorites! It is especially good when made with cucumbers fresh from the garden, but is also good with those from the local grocer.

his is a great way to get your kids to eat their broccoli! It is a delicious salad.

Cucumber Salad

2	cucumbers peeled and thinly sliced
1	cup mayonnaise
3	tablespoons sugar
3	tablespoons wine vinegar
2	teaspoons whole celery seed

Place sliced cucumbers in a bowl; cover with ice and chill thoroughly. Combine mayonnaise and remaining ingredients. Stir until well blended and creamy. Drain chilled cucumbers, add dressing, and stir until cucumbers are coated and serve.

Broccoli and Cauliflower Salad

1	head cauliflower, trimmed and cut into bite-size pieces
1	head fresh broccoli, trimmed and cut into bite-size pieces
½	cup sliced celery
¾	cup sliced stuffed olives
1	cup Cheddar cheese, cubed
1	(1-ounce) package dry Ranch dressing mix
¼	cup milk
½	cup sour cream

In a large bowl, combine cauliflower, broccoli, celery, olives, and cheese. In separate bowl, combine dressing mix, milk, and sour cream; whisk until creamy. Pour over vegetables, stir well to coat. Chill overnight.

Layered Salad

1	large head iceberg lettuce, shredded
½	cup chopped celery
½	cup frozen English peas, thawed
1	(1-ounce) package Ranch dressing mix prepared
2	tablespoons sour cream
2	cups Cheddar cheese, grated
4	strips bacon, fried and crumbled

This is an updated family favorite. For years, this salad was made with a heavy mayonnaise and sugar dressing. In an effort to find a salad that my children would eat, I substituted Ranch dressing for the mayonnaise. It worked, this is one salad they will eat by the bowlful!

The day before: Wash lettuce, wrap in paper towel. Place in zip-top plastic bag and chill. (This makes the lettuce crisp.) Cook peas according to package directions; drain and chill. Make Ranch dressing according to package directions, adding 2 tablespoons of sour cream. (Adding the sour cream thickens the dressing making it smooth and creamy.

Next day: Layer shredded lettuce in bottom of 9x13-inch glass dish. Next, layer celery and peas. Spoon on a thin layer of Ranch dressing to cover vegetables. Top with cheese then crumbled bacon.

Note: This salad is much better if assembled a short time before serving. Sprinkle bacon on minutes before serving to keep it from getting soggy.

Salads

A delicious luncheon salad, it is unique and flavorful.

Serving Suggestion: For an attractive presentation use an ice cream scoop to measure the salad then place each "scoop" on a lettuce leaf. Use an attractive leafy lettuce not the everyday iceberg variety. For a more gourmet look serve on a bed of the assorted European greens that are now available prepackaged at your local grocer.

Curried Chicken and Rice Salad

1½	cups cooked white rice
¼	cup minced onion
¼	cup diced green pepper
1	cup sliced celery
2	cups cooked chicken breasts, chopped
1	apple, unpeeled and chopped
½	teaspoon salt
½	teaspoon curry powder
2	tablespoons vegetable oil
¾	cup mayonnaise
1	tablespoon wine vinegar

Combine first 6 ingredients in a large bowl. Mix together next 5 ingredients then add to rice and chicken mixture. Mix well then refrigerate for several hours or until thoroughly chilled. Serve on a lettuce leaf.

Yield: 4 to 5 servings

Fresh Fruit Salad

1   cup orange segments
1   cup fresh pineapple chunks
1   cup fresh strawberry halves
1   cup cantaloupe chunks
1   cup watermelon chunks
1   cup grapefruit segments
1   cup seedless grape halves

Combine and chill. Serve with Hemphill's honey lime dressing.

Hemphill's Honey Lime Dressing

3   tablespoons lime juice
3   tablespoons honey
6   tablespoons salad oil
pinch   ginger
¼   teaspoon vinegar (or to taste)

Combine ingredients and shake well. Chill and serve over fresh fruit salad.

Salads

Ahh... Hemphill's fruit salad with honey lime dressing! Hemphill Wells Department Store was the essence of home town sophistication. It was Lubbock's own version of Neiman Marcus, just smaller. There in the "Gold Room," luncheons were hosted, business people met for lunch, and truck loads of fruit salad were served. There was something special about lunch at Hemphills. It was one of the last places where you could be embraced by a more civilized time. Sadly, Hemphills went the way of so many other hometown department stores and so went customer service and that wonderful salad.

79

Salads

*T*his is one of our favorite holiday salads. It is absolutely delicious! Our holiday meal would not be complete without it.

Royal Fruit Salad

1	(15 ¼-ounce) can pineapple chunks, drain, reserve juice
1	(16 ½-ounce) can Royal Anne cherries, drained
1	orange, sectioned and sliced into bite-size pieces
3	cups mini marshmallows
1	banana, sliced
1	Red Delicious apple unpeeled, cored and chopped
1	cup pecans, chopped

Dressing:

3	egg yolks
2	tablespoons sugar
2	tablespoons vinegar
2	tablespoons pineapple juice
1	tablespoon margarine
1	cup frozen whipped topping

In a saucepan, combine all dressing ingredients except whipped topping. Over low heat, cook until thickened. Remove from heat and cool to room temperature. While dressing is cooling, combine pineapple chunks, cherries, orange pieces, and marshmallows. Add whipped topping to dressing then pour over fruit; stir to coat fruit. Refrigerate overnight. Just before serving, add bananas, apples and pecans.

Note: If you add the bananas and apples too soon, they will turn dark. If pecans are added early, they will turn the salad dark.

Apricot Salad

1 (3-ounce) package peach jello
2 cups apricot nectar, divided
1 (3-ounce) package cream cheese
1 cup whipping cream, whipped
1 cup slivered almonds
1 (11-ounce) can Mandarin orange segments, drained

Dissolve gelatin in 1 cup of hot apricot nectar, stir in cream cheese until melted. Set aside to cool. Whip cream. Add whipped cream and remaining cup of apricot nectar to gelatin mixture. Beat to combine. Stir in almonds and orange segments. Pour into 1 quart mold; chill until set.

Yield: 6 servings

Note: If you use a jello mold be sure to spray lightly with nonstick cooking spray.

To unmold jello: first loosen edge with a knife (this releases the seal or vacuum), then dip in hot water for 5 seconds, and invert on a chilled plate. If time allows, return to refrigerator to firm up before serving.

I really don't know why this salad is called Apricot Salad. It is filled with so many wonderful ingredients like cream cheese, almonds, and Mandarin oranges. Whatever you want to call it... we call it delicious!

Note: If you do not have a gelatin mold just use an 8x8-inch glass dish.

81

Salads

A unique blend of flavors make this salad delicious!

Note: Spray your gelatin molds lightly with nonstick cooking spray before filling with the jello salad. This will make unmolding easier.

*T*he surprise is how good this combination of flavors can be!

Congealed Avocado Salad

1	(3-ounce) package lime jello
1	cup boiling water
1	(3-ounce) package cream cheese, softened
1	avocado, chopped
1	small onion, chopped fine
2	stalks celery, chopped
1	(2-ounce) jar diced pimento
½	cup mayonnaise

Dissolve jello in boiling water. Chill to syrupy stage. Combine softened cream cheese with remaining ingredients. Stir into cooled jello. Spoon into eight individual molds and chill until set. Serve on a lettuce leaf.

Surprise Gelatin Salad

1	(10 ¾-ounce) can tomato soup
1	(3-ounce) package cherry gelatin
½	cup chopped celery
½	cup chopped green pepper
½	cup chopped onion
1	cup cottage cheese
½	cup salad dressing
½	cup pecans, chopped

Heat soup; add gelatin. Remove from heat and stir until gelatin dissolves. Cool. Add remaining ingredients in order given and mix well. Pour into 8 individual gelatin molds and chill until firm.

Christmas Jello Salad

1	(6-ounce) package strawberry jello
1	(20-ounce) can crushed pineapple, undrained
1	cup sugar
3	tablespoons lemon juice
2	tablespoons unflavored gelatin
½	cup cold water
1	cup grated American cheese
½	pint whipping cream, whipped
2	tablespoons diced pimento
½	cup finely chopped pecans
1	(6-ounce) package lime jello
2	drops green food coloring

*N*aydiene often prepared this for a holiday meal. The red and green color makes it an especially attractive salad to serve at Christmas.

1st layer: Dissolve strawberry jello in 3½ cups boiling water. Pour into a 9x13-inch glass dish. Chill until firm.

2nd layer: Heat pineapple with juice, sugar, and lemon juice until sugar dissolves. Add unflavored gelatin that has been softened in ½ cup of cold water. Stir until dissolved. Cool mixture; add cheese, whipping cream, pimento, and pecans to pineapple mixture. Spread over red jello layer.

3rd layer: Prepare lime jello according to package directions. Add 2 drops of green food coloring to enhance color. Chill until syrupy; pour over pineapple-cheese layer and chill until set. Cut into squares.

Yield: 15 servings

Salads

classic family favorite for generations! I am sure your grand-mother made this salad as often as mine did. Still a favorite today, it's pretty red color brightens any plate!

Note: Partially congealed jello will have the consistency of egg whites. Allowing the jello mixture to partially congeal keeps the pieces of fruit and pecans from sinking to the bottom.

Grandmother West's Cherry Salad

½	cup cherry juice
½	cup pineapple juice
1	(3-ounce) package cherry jello
1	(12-ounce) cola flavored drink, chilled
1	cup crushed pineapple, drained
1	cup Bing cherries, drained and chopped
1	cup finely chopped pecans

In a saucepan, combine cherry and pineapple juice; bring to a boil. Add cherry jello; stir until dissolved. Chill until partially congealed. Stir in cola, pineapple, cherries, and pecans. Pour into an 8x8-inch glass dish. Chill until firm. To serve, cut into squares.

Yield: 9 servings

Cherry Pecan Salad

1	(16-ounce) can red, sour, pitted cherries with juice
½	cup sugar
½	teaspoon red food coloring
1	(13-ounce) can pineapple tidbits with juice
1	(3-ounce) package cherry jello
½	teaspoon almond extract
1	tablespoon fresh lemon juice
1	cup chopped pecans

Pour cherries and juice into a saucepan, add sugar and food coloring. Bring to a boil; reduce heat and cook slowly for 10 minutes, stirring occasionally. Drain well, reserving juice. Measure reserved cherry juice, juice from pineapple, and enough water to make 2 cups. Bring to a boil and pour over jello. Stir until jello dissolves. Add almond extract and lemon juice. Refrigerate until partially congealed; stir in cherries, pineapple and pecans. Pour into an 8x8-inch glass dish or 8 individual jello molds. Chill until set.

Yield: 8 servings

Another family favorite, Naydiene often made this salad.

Note: Spray your jello molds lightly with non stick cooking spray. Your salad will slip right out! Be sure to just spray the mold lightly. Too much nonstick cooking spray will make your jello look cloudy.

85

Salads

*C*ranberry relish is one of those time tested dishes that has been around forever. It is a natural compliment to turkey or chicken and is much better than canned cranberry sauce.

*I*f you like cranberry relish, you will love this jello salad! Naydiene always used an old fashion grinder but you can use your food processor. Just pulse it a few times so the cranberries and oranges are coarsely ground.

Cranberry Relish

1	pound fresh cranberries, washed and drained
2	large navel oranges
2	cups sugar
pinch	salt

Grind cranberries and orange peel. Finely chop orange pulp. Combine fruit with sugar and salt. Stir until well combined. Chill completely before serving. Will keep in refrigerator for a week or more.

Note: Flavor improves as the ingredients have time to blend together so prepare a day or 2 ahead of serving.

Cranberry Jello Salad

1	(14-ounce) package fresh cranberries, coarsely ground
2	oranges with peel, ground
2	apples, ground (core but leave peeling)
2	cups sugar
1	(3-ounce) package cherry jello
1	cup hot water
1	cup chopped pecans

In a large bowl, combine ground cranberries, oranges, and apples. Pour on sugar; set aside. Dissolve jello in hot water, add to fruit mixture. Stir in pecans. Pour into an 8x8-inch glass dish. Chill until set. Cut into squares to serve.

Grandmother's
Apple Ginger Ale Salad

1	(3-ounce) package lime jello
2	cups ginger ale, divided
2	(3-ounce) packages cream cheese
2	large Rome apples, peeled and grated
pinch	salt
1	tablespoon lemon juice
1	(10-ounce) jar Maraschino cherries without stems, drained and halved

Dissolve lime gelatin in 1 cup of hot ginger ale. Blend together cream cheese, 1 cup of ginger ale, grated apples, salt, lemon juice, and cherries. Stir into gelatin/ginger ale mixture then pour into gelatin mold or 8x8-inch glass dish. Chill until set.

Yield: 8 servings

An attractive accompaniment to a luncheon plate. This recipe also came from my Grandmother West.

Serving Suggestion: Cut into squares and serve on a lettuce leaf. Use a pretty leafy lettuce.

87

Salads

*T*his delicious salad is always a favorite.

Note: When it says chill to semi-set, the jello will have the consistency of egg whites.

Grand Prairie Salad

1	(3-ounce) package lime jello
2	cups boiling water
20	miniature marshmallows
1	cup grated American cheese
1	(8-ounce) can crushed pineapple, drained
1	cup pecans, chopped
½	pint whipping cream, whipped

Dissolve jello in boiling water; add marshmallows. Boil slowly, stirring until marshmallows dissolve. Chill until semi-set but not firm. Add cheese, pineapple, and pecans. Fold in whipped cream; stir until well mixed. Pour into 8x8-inch glass dish or jello mold. Chill until set.

Yield: 8 servings

Note: Naydiene usually made this in an 8x8-inch dish. She then cut the jello salad into squares and served on a lettuce leaf.

Naydiene's Jello

1   (6-ounce) package jello
     (flavor of your choice)
4   cups boiling water
1   handful miniature
     marshmallows

Pour jello in a large bowl. Bring water to a boil; add marshmallows. Stir until marshmallows dissolve. Pour over jello and stir until dissolved. Put in an 8x8-inch glass dish; chill until set.

Note: This method takes a little longer but the results are "clearly" delicious! Do not microwave the water, it just does not get hot enough and will make your jello cloudy.

If you want to add fruit to this jello, partially congeal it before stirring in the fruit. This will keep the fruit from sinking to the bottom.

*O*nly Naydiene could improve on something as simple as jello. Two simple things: boiling all 4 cups of your water and adding marshmallows will have your family and guests saying, "This is the best jello I have ever tasted!"

Serving Suggestion: Naydiene often made this jello in a jello mold when she had guests for Sunday lunch. She would serve it on a large plate surrounded by fresh fruit. This was always a favorite with the grandchildren and of course they requested red jello!

Salads

*B*oth of these salads are pretty and delicious. They each make a nice addition to a luncheon plate or a special Sunday dinner.

A wonderful combination of flavors and ingredients!

Aunt Marge's Orange Jello Salad

1	(3-ounce) package orange jello
½	cup boiling water
1	cup whipping cream
1	(8-ounce) can crushed pineapple with juice
½	cup chopped pecans
½	cup grated American cheese

Dissolve gelatin in boiling water. Cool until room temperature; stir in remaining ingredients. Transfer to 8x8-inch glass dish. Chill until set.

Orange Ambrosia Salad

1	(3-ounce) package orange jello
½	cup sugar
1	cup hot water
3	oranges, peeled and cut into 1-inch pieces
1	(8-ounce) can crushed pineapple, undrained
1	cup flake coconut
1	cup chopped pecans
1	(8-ounce) carton sour cream

Dissolve jello in hot water. Cool, then stir in remaining ingredients. Pour into a 9x13-inch glass dish. Chill until set. Cut into squares.

Jello Pear Salad

1   (16-ounce) can pear halves in syrup
1   (3-ounce) package cherry jello
1   cup boiling water
1   (4½-ounce) carton whipped topping, thawed

Drain pear halves, reserving syrup. Measure syrup and enough water to make 1 cup. Dissolve gelatin in boiling water; stir in measured liquid. Chill until thickened. Dice pears and set aside. Fold ½ cup of thickened gelatin into whipped topping. If necessary, chill mixture again so it will mound. Spoon gelatin mixture into a shallow serving bowl; mound high at edges to form a shell. Add diced pears to remaining thickened gelatin; carefully spoon into middle of "shell." Chill until jello is set.

Yield: 8 to 10 servings

My sister, Karen, often prepares this very attractive and delicious salad for our family gatherings.

Note: This salad looks especially pretty in a glass or crystal serving bowl.

Salads

*M*y aunt, Bettye Jo Wiley, first brought this salad to a West family gathering. It quickly became a family favorite. I remember my Grandmother West often served this salad at Thanksgiving. Now the great grandchildren expect it for every holiday. My mom is always happy to oblige. The only problem is they only want to eat the salad and none of the turkey and dressing!

Strawberry ~ Pretzel Salad

Crust:

1½	cups crushed pretzels
1½	sticks margarine, softened
3	tablespoons sugar

2nd Layer:

1	(8-ounce) package cream cheese
1	cup sugar
1	(8-ounce) carton whipped topping

3rd Layer:

1	(6-ounce) package strawberry jello
2	(10-ounce) packages frozen strawberries, thawed

Combine crushed pretzels, softened margarine and sugar; stir until well mixed. Press into bottom of 9x13-inch glass baking dish. Bake at 350° for 10 to 15 minutes; cool completely. Combine cream cheese and 1 cup sugar. Blend until smooth. Fold in whipped topping; spread over cooled crust. Refrigerate. Dissolve jello in 2 cups hot water. Add ½ cup cold water. Stir in strawberries. Chill until partially firm. Pour over cream cheese layer. Chill overnight. To serve, cut into squares.

Yield: 12 to 15 servings

Hint: Place pretzels in a heavy plastic zip-top bag and use a rolling pin to crush, then toss the bag for easy cleanup.

Main Dishes

Family Ties

Family ties are precious things
woven through the years.
Of memories of togetherness
of laughter, love and tears.

Family ties are cherished things
forged in childhood days,
By love of parents deep and true
and sweet familiar ways.

Family ties are treasured things
and far though we may roam,
The tender bonds with those
we love still pull our hearts
toward home.

Author Unknown

Sunday Lunch at Naydiene's

One of the things I remember most (and my husband misses the most), is Naydiene's Sunday lunch. On Sunday, Naydiene would "put the little pot in the big pot" and fill our table with a delightful array of food. Her food was not gourmet, just good old-fashioned home cooking, rich in her Southern tradition.

There was always a main dish and several bowls brimming with fresh vegetables, a salad or two, bread, and of course, dessert. They were all served in a variety of pretty bowls. Some were china painted by relatives and others were pretty, antique, colored-glass bowls that were family heirlooms, others were pieces she had collected. The food was always served family style. As it was being passed, my children would fill their plates with things you think kids would never eat, like stewed okra, baked squash, and black-eyed peas. The kids called her cooking *real* food. They would gobble it up as if they hadn't eaten in a week and the reality was they had not eaten food like this since last Sunday! Of course my husband loved it. I found it totally amazing that one woman could prepare so much wonderful food with such ease and grace.

Naydiene was also the perfect hostess, always jumping up to fill your tea glass before you even knew it was empty and encouraging us to eat more because she did not want any leftovers! The time we spent around the table with my husband's parents, Otis and Naydiene, was always a time to relax and refresh ourselves after a hectic week. It was like Sundays past, when family and faith took center stage and everyone stopped for a moment to give thanks. It was the way Sunday lunch was meant to be!

Mom's Brisket
"Easy to prepare!"

5 to 6 pound trimmed brisket
⅓   cup liquid smoke
2   teaspoons onion powder
2   teaspoons celery salt
2   teaspoons garlic powder
salt and pepper to taste
1   tablespoon Worcestershire sauce
¾   cup barbeque sauce

Place brisket in a broiler pan. Pour liquid smoke over brisket. Sprinkle with onion powder, garlic powder, and celery salt. Cover with foil and refrigerate over night. Next day, pour on Worcestershire sauce and sprinkle with salt and pepper. Cover and put in a 275° oven for 5 hours. Remove from oven, and cover with your favorite barbeque sauce. Cook 1 hour longer. Warm additional sauce and serve with brisket.

Great served with Country Baked Beans (page 129) and Creamy Potato Salad (page 70)!

Main Dishes

Quick idea for leftover brisket: Top baked potatoes with chopped brisket, grated Cheddar cheese, barbeque sauce, and salt and pepper. Our whole family enjoys this quick meal.

Tips for microwave baked potatoes:
Wash baking potatoes, pat dry with paper towel, and prick several times with a fork. Wrap in plastic wrap and microwave on high for about 15 to 20 minutes (if cooking 4 potatoes). When the potatoes feel soft, remove from microwave. Take off plastic wrap and wrap in foil. Let sit 15 minutes then serve.

Main Dishes

*E*ven though this is called a stew, it is served in a casserole dish and the vegetables are cut into much larger chunks. By cooking the meat and vegetables separately, they remain firm and are not mushy like they can become in a regular stew.

Serving Suggestion: Combine this dish with a pan of cornbread and you have the perfect meal for a cool autumn evening.

Naydiene's Favorite Stew

2	pounds lean beef cubed (1½-inch cubes)
2	tablespoons olive oil
1½	cups tomato juice
½	cup water
1½	teaspoons salt
8	carrots sliced lengthwise and cut in 2-inch lengths
3 to 4	medium onions, quartered
4 to 6	medium potatoes, peeled and cut into chunks
8	celery stalks, cut in 2-inch lengths
1	tablespoon cornstarch
1	tablespoon sugar
1	cup cooking wine

Brown meat cubes on all sides in olive oil. Add tomato juice, water, and salt. Cook for an hour over medium heat or until meat is tender. Remove meat and cook vegetables in same broth until they are almost tender. Combine cooked vegetables and cooked stew meat in a covered baking dish. Mix remaining tomato/beef broth, cornstarch, sugar, and wine; bring to a boil. Pour over meat and vegetables and bake for 35 minutes at 350°.

Yield: 6 to 8 servings

Spanish Round Steak

2   pounds round steak
⅓   cup flour
salt and pepper to taste
¼   cup oil
1   teaspoon cumin
1   teaspoon sugar
1   (15-ounce) can tomato sauce
½   cup water
1   tablespoon lemon juice
1   teaspoon garlic powder
1   beef bouillon cube dissolved
         in ½ cup boiling water
½   cup chopped green pepper
½   cup chopped onion
1   (4-ounce) can chopped green
         chilies

A mild dish with a great southwestern flavor! While the meat is simmering in the sauce, prepare the rice and a salad for a quick meal.

Cut steak into thin strips. Dredge strips in flour seasoned with salt and pepper. Pour oil in a skillet and brown meat on all sides (I like to use an electric skillet). Pour off the drippings. Add the rest of the ingredients and stir until well blended. Simmer, covered for 30 to 40 minutes stirring occasionally. Serve over white rice.

Main Dishes

A quick, easy, and elegant main dish.

Note: When cooking pasta, add salt to the boiling water for flavor. Also, adding one tablespoon of olive or vegetable oil to the water keeps the pasta from sticking together while cooking. It also keeps the water from boiling over!

For variety, serve over whole wheat or spinach noodles.

Easy Beef Stroganoff

2	pounds round steak
½	cup flour
salt and pepper to taste	
1	green pepper, chopped
½	onion, chopped
1	(10 ¾-ounce) can cream of mushroom soup
1	(4.5-ounce) jar sliced mushrooms with liquid
¼	teaspoon garlic powder
1	(8-ounce) carton sour cream
1	(10-ounce) package wide egg noodles

Cut round steak into thin strips. Salt and pepper steak strips then dredge in flour. In a large skillet, brown meat slowly in a small amount of vegetable oil (cook about 20 minutes). Remove meat and set aside. In the same skillet, sauté green pepper and onion. Stir in soup, mushrooms with liquid, and garlic powder. Add meat and stir. Simmer until meat is warm and sauce is bubbly. Stir in sour cream. When sauce is hot throughout, serve over cooked wide noodles.

Mom's Meat Loaf

2	pounds lean ground beef
2	eggs, slightly beaten
1½	cups cracker crumbs
¾	cup ketchup
1	teaspoon seasoned salt
½	cup warm water
1	package dry onion soup mix
1	(4-ounce) can tomato sauce

Combine all ingredients. Mix thoroughly. Press into a loaf pan that has been sprayed with nonstick cooking spray. Refrigerate overnight or cook immediately . When ready to cook, top with tomato sauce. Bake at 350° for 1½ hours. Drain off excess fat. Let set 10 to 15 minutes before serving.

Yield: 8 servings

Note: Ground round is a good choice for making meat loaf. It is lower in fat than regular ground beef yet has enough fat to keep your meat loaf from being dry. I also prefer using fresh ground beef instead of beef that has been frozen.

Main Dishes

lways a family favorite! Meat loaf is the ultimate "comfort food." It is the perfect mate for scalloped or mashed potatoes (page 140).

Main Dishes

*C*reamy noodles and a flavorful meat sauce make this casserole delicious!

Note: This casserole freezes well.

Helpful Hints: When cooking noodles add 1 tablespoon salt to the boiling water; this will enhance the flavor of the noodles. Also, add 1 tablespoon of olive oil or vegetable oil in the water. This keeps the water from boiling over.

Beef Noodle Casserole

2	pounds ground beef
½	cup chopped onion
1	cup chopped green pepper
2	teaspoons garlic powder
1	tablespoon sugar
2	tablespoons Worcestershire sauce
1	(15-ounce) can tomato sauce
	salt and pepper to taste
1	(10-ounce) package wide egg noodles
1	(8-ounce) package cream cheese, softened
1	(8-ounce) carton sour cream
3	green onions, chopped
1	cup grated Cheddar cheese

In a large skillet, brown ground beef; drain. Add onion and green pepper; cook slowly until vegetables are tender. Add garlic powder, sugar, Worcestershire, and tomato sauce. Add salt and pepper to taste. Simmer for about 20 minutes. While meat sauce is simmering, cook noodles in boiling salted water according to package directions. Drain noodles. Place hot noodles in a bowl with the cream cheese and sour cream. Stir until noodles are coated. Add green onions if your family likes them. In a lightly greased baking dish, layer ½ the noodle mixture and ½ the meat mixture. Repeat. Top with grated Cheddar cheese. Bake in a 350° oven for 20 to 30 minutes.

Rosemary Beef Casserole

1	(12-ounce) package shell macaroni
¼	stick of butter or margarine
1	pound ground beef
½	cup diced onion
¾	cup diced celery
1	(8-ounce) can tomato sauce
1	teaspoon salt
½	teaspoon pepper
¼	teaspoon garlic salt
1	teaspoon pepper sauce
2	teaspoons Worcestershire sauce
1	teaspoon dried rosemary flakes
1	teaspoon parsley flakes
1	cup evaporated milk
1	(10 ¾-ounce) can cream of mushroom soup, undiluted
1½	cups grated Cheddar cheese

Prepare macaroni in boiling salted water according to package directions. In a large skillet, sauté ground beef in butter until brown; drain. Add onion and celery, saute until tender. Add tomato sauce and next 7 ingredients. Simmer, stirring occasionally. In a saucepan, heat milk, soup, and cheese until cheese is melted. Pour soup mixture into skillet with beef. Add drained macaroni and stir well. Pour into a 9x13-inch glass dish that has been sprayed with nonstick cooking spray. Sprinkle with additional grated cheese. Bake at 350° for 30 to 40 minutes.

Main Dishes

The rosemary makes this everyday beef and noodle casserole extra special.

For a variation of this casserole, use a 15-ounce can of tomato sauce instead of the 8-ounce and sprinkle finely shredded Parmesan cheese on top instead of Cheddar. This gives the casserole a different flavor... more Italian!

Note: This casserole freezes well. When freezing a casserole, I normally leave the cheese off the top. It works better to sprinkle the cheese on during the reheating process.

Main Dishes

*M*y kids always ask for "more" of this casserole. It is easy to make and freezes well.

I am intrigued by the Once-A-Month cooking trend and have tried it especially during baseball season! Many of the casseroles in this section freeze well. Naydiene, always had an extra casserole or two in her freezer. She was always ready for an unplanned event or unexpected company!

Time-Saving Tip: Thaw frozen casseroles in your refrigerator overnight. This cuts the reheating time in half!

More Casserole

1	(5-ounce) package of egg noodles
1	pound ground beef
½	cup chopped onion
½	cup chopped green pepper
1	cup chopped celery
1	(8-ounce) can tomato sauce
1	(12-ounce) can of corn
1	tablespoon of chili powder
1	teaspoon salt
½	teaspoon pepper
1	cup grated Cheddar cheese

Cook noodles in boiling salted water according to package directions. In a large skillet, brown ground beef and drain. Add onion, green pepper, and celery. Cook slowly for several minutes until vegetables are tender. Add drained noodles, tomato sauce, corn, chili powder, salt, and pepper. Mix well. Pour into a greased 9x13-inch casserole dish. Top with grated cheese. Bake uncovered at 350° for 20 to 30 minutes.

Yield: 8-10 servings

Lasagna

2	pounds ground beef
1	teaspoon California-style garlic powder
¾	teaspoon oregano
2	teaspoons seasoned salt
¼	teaspoon fresh ground pepper
1	package dry spaghetti sauce mix
1	(15-ounce) can tomato sauce
1	(8-ounce) can tomato sauce
1	cup water
12	lasagna noodles

Brown ground beef; drain. Add garlic powder, oregano, salt, and pepper. Stir well. Simmer a few minutes then add spaghetti sauce mix, tomato sauce, and water. Cover and simmer approximately 20 minutes. While sauce is simmering, prepare the lasagna noodles in boiling, salted water according to package directions. Drain and lay flat to cool. In a large bowl, combine ricotta, cheeses, eggs, parsley, salt, and pepper. To assemble, spray a 9x13-inch glass dish with nonstick cooking spray. Spread ½ cup of meat sauce in bottom of dish. Lay 4 noodles lengthwise over sauce overlapping edges. Spread ½ of cheese mixture over noodles and top with 1 cup of the meat sauce. Repeat layers ending with noodles. Top with remaining meat sauce. Sprinkle with additional Parmesan cheese. Cover with foil and bake in a 350° oven for 35 to 40 minutes. Remove foil; bake an additional 10 minutes. Let stand 10 minutes before serving.

Main Dishes

Lasagna does take extra time to prepare, but since it freezes well you can make it in advance. Now you are ready for guests! All you need to add is a salad and French bread for a complete meal.

Filling:

1	(15-ounce) carton ricotta cheese
2	cups grated Italian Blend cheese (available at your local grocer)
¼	cup finely shredded Parmesan cheese
2	eggs
1	tablespoon dried parsley flakes
1	teaspoon salt
¼	teaspoon fresh ground pepper

Variation: For a little spice use half Italian sausage and half ground beef.

Main Dishes

nother quick and easy favorite! This has a great flavor and is mild enough to please the entire family. Serve with a green salad or guacamole.

Time-Saving Hint: Use prepackaged grated cheese. Try a package of Mexican blend cheese for a great flavor!

Mexican Dinner

2	pounds ground beef
½	onion, chopped
1	(10-ounce) can mild enchilada sauce
1	(10 ¾-ounce) can cream of mushroom soup
1	(10 ¾-ounce) can cream of chicken soup
1	(7-ounce) can green chilies
1	package corn tortillas
1	cup grated Cheddar cheese

Brown meat and onion in a large skillet; drain well. Add remaining ingredients except tortillas and cheese. Stir until well combined then simmer until bubbly and heated throughout. Quarter tortillas. Spray a 9x13-inch baking dish with nonstick spray. Line bottom of dish with tortillas. Layer with meat mixture, repeat layers and top with cheese. Bake at 350° for 20 to 30 minutes or until cheese is melted and casserole is bubbly.

Yield: 10-12 servings

Tijuana Torte

"Stacked enchiladas"

1	pound ground beef
1	medium onion, chopped
1	(15-ounce) can tomato sauce
1	(4-ounce) can chopped green chilies
1	package taco seasoning mix
12	corn tortillas
1	pound Cheddar cheese, grated

*T*hese stacked enchiladas are also quick and easy. Add a green salad for a complete meal.

Brown ground beef and onion. Drain well. Add tomato sauce, green chilies, and seasoning mix. Stir until well combined then simmer 10 to 15 minutes. Place about ¼ cup meat mixture in the bottom of a 9x13-inch baking dish. Place two tortillas side by side on the meat mixture; sprinkle with grated cheese. Continue layering until each stack has 6 tortillas layered with meat and cheese. Bake at 350° for 20 to 25 minutes or until bubbly. Let set 5 minutes. Cut each stack into quarters with a sharp knife before serving.

Yield: 8 servings

Serving Suggestion: Top with sour cream and a slice of avocado if you like.

105

Main Dishes

Southwestern flavor and corn tortillas make this a unique and tasty lasagna!

Note: This casserole does *not* freeze well. The tortillas tend to get mushy.

Southwestern Lasagna

2	pounds ground beef
½	onion, chopped
1	clove garlic, minced
2	tablespoons chili powder
1	(15-ounce) can tomato sauce
1	(8-ounce) can tomato sauce
1	teaspoon sugar
1	teaspoon salt
1	(4-ounce) can chopped green chilies
2	cups small curd cottage cheese
1	egg, beaten
1	pound Monterey Jack cheese, grated
12	corn tortillas, cut in fourths
1	cup grated cheddar cheese
½	cup chopped black olives

Brown ground beef; drain. Add onion and garlic, cook until soft. Stir in chili powder. Add tomato sauce, sugar, salt, and green chilies. Simmer about 15 minutes. Blend together cottage cheese and egg; set aside. Spray a 9x13-inch glass pan with nonstick cooking spray. Layer ⅓ meat mixture, ½ Monterey Jack cheese, ½ cottage cheese mixture and ½ tortillas. Repeat, ending with meat sauce. Top with grated Cheddar cheese and black olives. Bake for 30 minutes at 350°.

Green Chile Beef Enchiladas

1 (10 ¾-ounce) can cream of chicken soup
1 small can evaporated milk
½ pound processed cheese
1 (4-ounce) can chopped green chilies
1 (4-ounce) jar diced pimentos
1 pound ground beef
½ onion, chopped
salt and pepper to taste
½ pound Longhorn Style Cheddar cheese, grated
1 dozen corn tortillas

We love green chiles at our house so these enchiladas are a favorite.

Heat soup, milk, and processed cheese in double boiler until melted. Add green chilies and pimentos. Brown ground beef and onions; drain well. Combine meat, onions, salt, pepper and Longhorn cheese. Fill each tortilla with meat mixture. Roll tightly and place seam side down in a greased 9x13-inch casserole dish. Pour cheese sauce over enchiladas. Cover with foil and bake at 350° for 30 minutes. Remove foil and bake an additional 5 minutes. Top with sour cream if desired.

Time-Saving Tip: Remember the kids can help with dinner. Let them set the table, prepare the salad, and fill tea or water glasses. They can also help with the clean up too!

Main Dishes

*D*ell Burgers are a summertime favorite. My sister, Karen, and many of our friends, say they are the best burgers around!

To warm hamburger buns, simply wrap in aluminum foil and heat in a low oven while the burgers are cooking.

*O*ur favorite version of Dell Burgers includes homemade hickory sauce. Who knew it was so easy to make!

Dell Burgers

2¼ pounds lean ground round
⅓ cup "Woody's" Cook-in Sauce
salt and fresh ground pepper to taste
6 large hamburger buns

Thoroughly mix in cook-in sauce, salt and pepper; this usually requires using your hands! Make out into large, thick, 6-ounce patties. Slowly grill on a charcoal or gas grill until patties are medium-well done. A few minutes before removing from the grill, melt a thick slice of Longhorn Style Cheddar cheese on each patty. Serve on warm hamburger buns with your favorite trimmings.

"Woody's" cook-in sauce is available in most areas at your local grocery. It will be found in the sauce and condiment section.

Hickory Sauce

½ cup ketchup
1 tablespoon Liquid Smoke

Combine ingredients until well blended. Serve on Dell Burgers. Add strips of cooked bacon for a delicious Hickory Bacon Cheeseburger.

South of the Border Chicken

6	boneless, skinless chicken breasts
3	eggs, beaten
5	tablespoons picante sauce
1½	cups dry bread crumbs
2	tablespoons chili powder
2	teaspoons cumin
1	teaspoon California-style garlic powder
⅓	cup margarine

Preheat oven to 375°. Combine eggs and picante sauce in a bowl. In another bowl or plate, combine bread crumbs and seasonings. Line a 9x13-inch glass baking dish with foil. Melt margarine in foil-lined dish. Salt and pepper chicken breasts then dip in the egg mixture and dredge in the seasoned bread crumbs. Place chicken in dish with melted butter, turn over to coat both sides. Bake uncovered for 30 minutes or until lightly brown and cooked throughout. Serve each piece topped with a thin slice of avocado, a dollop of sour cream, picante sauce, grated Cheddar cheese, and diced green onion.

This is such an attractive dish! Serve with Spanish Rice (page 124) and Napa Green Salad (page 74). Delicious! Plus, with the foil-lined pan, cleanup is a breeze.

Note: You can prepare chicken ahead of time; then place in the oven right before your guests arrive.

Main Dishes

*M*y absolute favorite Chicken Enchiladas! The sour cream sauce is simple to make and has a great flavor.

Note: Work on wax paper when filling and rolling tortillas for easy cleanup.

Sour Cream Chicken Enchiladas

4	boneless, skinless chicken breasts cooked and finely chopped
½	onion, chopped
¼	cup butter
¼	cup flour
2½	cups water
3	chicken bouillon cubes
1	(8-ounce) carton sour cream
2	cups grated Cheddar cheese, divided
1	(4-ounce) can chopped green chilies, drained
1	(2-ounce) jar of diced pimentos (optional)
½	teaspoon chili powder
	salt and pepper to taste
10-12	8-inch flour tortillas

Saute onion in butter until soft and transparent. Add flour; stir until well blended and makes a paste. Add water and bouillon cubes. Bring to a boil. Cook over medium heat until sauce thickens, stirring occasionally. Remove from heat and stir in sour cream. Set aside. In a bowl, combine 1 cup of sauce, chopped chicken, 1 cup of Cheddar cheese, green chilies, pimiento, chili powder, salt, and pepper. Dip tortillas in sauce to soften. Spoon chicken mixture down center of tortilla and roll up. Place in a greased 9x13-inch glass dish, seam side down. Continue process until dish is full. Cover with remaining sauce and sprinkle with remaining cheese. Cook at 350° until bubbly.

Grilled Cumin and Cayenne Chicken

6	boneless, skinless chicken breasts
6	tablespoons extra-virgin olive oil
3	teaspoons ground cumin
2	teaspoons ground thyme
1	teaspoon fresh ground black pepper
½	teaspoon cayenne
½	teaspoon salt

Combine olive oil, spices, and salt; preferably 1 or 2 hours ahead of time so the flavors can mingle. Lay chicken breasts in a shallow pan and cover with ¾ oil mixture. Allow chicken to marinade in the refrigerator for at least 2 hours. Place chicken breasts on grill. Cover and cook for 4 minutes on each side or until juices run clear. Use reserved marinade to baste each breast liberally before and after turning.

Yield: 6 servings

Hint: Use leftover chicken to make a great Grilled Chicken Salad!

Main Dishes

The combination of spices in this marinade blend well with the smoky flavor obtained by grilling over a charcoal or gas grill. If you use a gas grill, you can still achieve a wonderful smoky flavor by wrapping several chunks of hard wood in aluminum foil. Pierce the foil pouch so the smoke can escape, then place the pouch over the fire, below the meat. Be sure and soak the wood in water before wrapping in foil. We love the sweet smoke of mesquite wood, but any hard wood or fruit wood will do. Experiment with several woods, because the flavors are noticeably different.

Main Dishes

A Sunday lunch favorite. This is delicious served with Naydiene's Baked Rice (page 123).

Note: Cut the chicken breasts in half if they are large. You want each piece to be one serving.

Dell's Favorite Chicken

6	boneless, skinless chicken breasts
	salt and pepper to taste
6	slices of bacon
1	(4-ounce) jar of sliced dried beef
1	(10 ¾-ounce) can cream of mushroom soup, undiluted
1	(8-ounce) carton sour cream

Season chicken with salt and pepper. Wrap each chicken breast with bacon. Spray a 9x13-inch baking dish with nonstick cooking spray. Cover bottom of dish with dried beef. Place chicken on top of beef. Combine soup and sour cream. Spoon on top of chicken. Bake at 275° covered for 1½ hours. Uncover and cook an additional hour or until chicken has cooked throughout.

Yield: 6 servings

Susan's Chicken Pot Pie

3	large boneless, skinless chicken breasts
4	medium potatoes, pared and cut into 1-inch chunks
1	cup sliced celery
1	cup sliced carrots
1	(8.5-ounce) can tiny English peas
½	cup butter or margarine
⅔	cup flour
1	cup milk
1	chicken bouillon cube
2	teaspoons salt
½	teaspoon pepper
Pastry for a double-crust, 9-inch pie	

*A*nother favorite "comfort food." Chicken Pot Pie always reminds me of home!

Time-Saving Tip: I find it saves time to use the boneless chicken breasts instead of cooking a whole chicken and deboning it.

Cook chicken; cool and cut into bite-size pieces. Set aside. Prepare potatoes, celery, and carrots. Place in broth left from cooking chicken; simmer until tender. Drain vegetables, reserving 3 cups broth. Combine chicken, cooked vegetables, and peas, place in a 9x13-inch casserole dish that has been sprayed with nonstick cooking spray. Melt butter in a saucepan over low heat; add flour and stir until smooth. Gradually stir in milk, chicken broth, and add bouillon cube. Cook over medium heat, stirring until thick and bubbly. Add salt and pepper. Pour the sauce over chicken and vegetables. Prepare pastry (I use Mom's pastry recipe (page 164). Roll out pastry to fit over casserole. Place on top of chicken mixture, cut slits in crust so steam can escape. Bake at 400° for 45 minutes or until crust is golden brown.

For variety place crust in bottom of casserole dish. Combine chicken, vegetables, and sauce; pour over crust. Top with additional crust. Be creative, use leaf or chicken cookie cutters to cut out extra pastry and place on top!

Main Dishes

Quick and easy!
You can control how
spicy this casserole is
by the type of salsa
used. For extra variety
and flavor, experiment
with some of the new
salsas like chipolte.

Note: Using plain
Velveeta will also make
this a milder casserole.

Spicy Chicken Lasagna

1	(10 ¾-ounce) can cream of chicken soup
8	ounces mild Mexican Velveeta
½	teaspoon cumin
2	cups cooked, chopped chicken breasts
1	(7-ounce) can chopped green chilies
10	corn tortillas, cut into strips
1	cup mild chunky style salsa, divided

In a saucepan melt together the soup, cheese, and cumin. Stir in cooked chicken and green chilies, Spread ¼ of chicken mixture into a 9x13-inch casserole dish that has been sprayed with nonstick cooking spray. Top with tortilla strips and ⅓ cup of salsa. Repeat layers ending with chicken mixture. Bake at 350° for 30 minutes. Top with a few remaining tortilla strips and cook an additional 10 minutes. Serve with additional salsa.

Note: I use boneless, skinless chicken breasts. The brand I purchase has been individually frozen. I find these to be tender and juicy. For the casseroles in this cookbook, the chicken breasts are cooked in salted boiling water until cooked throughout. This generally takes 25 to 30 minutes.

Chicken, Wild Rice and Almond Casserole

Main Dishes

4	large boneless, skinless chicken breasts, cooked and cut into bite-size pieces
1	box fast cooking wild rice with herbs, prepared in 2½ cups of chicken broth
1	(15-ounce) can French-style green beans, drained
1	cup Hellman's mayonnaise
1	(2-ounce) jar diced pimento
1	(10 ¾-ounce) can cream of celery soup, undiluted
1	cup sliced or slivered almonds
	salt and pepper to taste
½	cup finely shredded Parmesan cheese
¼	teaspoon paprika

A family favorite, this casserole has it all! It is a great one-dish meal. Plus it is quick and easy to make.

Note: There is no substitute for fresh Parmesan cheese. You can grate your own or buy it prepackaged at your local grocer. Look for the kind that says finely shredded not the grated type in the can.

Combine cooked chicken, prepared rice, green beans, mayonnaise, pimentos, celery soup, and almonds. Mix thoroughly. Season to taste with salt and pepper. Place in a 9x13-inch casserole dish that has been sprayed with nonstick cooking spray. Top casserole generously with Parmesan cheese and sprinkle lightly with paprika. Bake uncovered in a 350° oven for 20 to 30 minutes or until bubbly.

Main Dishes

*M*y kids love this casserole and I like that it combines chicken and broccoli into a great one dish meal.

Chicken Divan

12-15	broccoli spears, cooked tender
3	large boneless, skinless chicken breasts, cooked and cut into bite-size pieces
1	(10 ¾-ounce) can cream of chicken soup
1	cup Hellman's mayonnaise
1	teaspoon lemon juice
½	teaspoon curry powder
½	cup Cheddar cheese
½	cup bread crumbs
1	teaspoon butter, melted

Spray a 9x13-inch casserole dish with nonstick cooking spray. Lay broccoli spears with florets facing outside edge of dish. (This makes a more attractive casserole.) Sprinkle half of cubed chicken on top of broccoli. Combine soup, mayonnaise, lemon juice, and curry powder. Spread on top of broccoli. Top with remaining chicken and grated Cheddar cheese. Toss bread crumbs in the melted butter until coated. Spoon crumbs over casserole. Bake uncovered at 350° for 30 minutes. Serve with wild rice.

Yield: 6 servings

Cheesy Chicken Tetrazzini

4	boneless, skinless chicken breasts, cooked
1	(7-ounce) package spaghetti
¼	cup margarine or butter
1	medium green pepper, chopped
2½	tablespoons flour
1	cup milk
1	(10 ¾-ounce) can cream of celery soup
1	(2-ounce) jar diced pimento
⅛	teaspoon garlic powder
¼	cup white cooking wine
1	(4-ounce) can sliced mushrooms, drained
½	cup finely shredded Parmesan cheese
3	cups, shredded American cheese, divided
	salt and pepper to taste
½	cup sliced almonds

A great blend of flavors. This is one of my husband's favorites.

This casserole also freezes well.

Note: I often use grated Cheddar cheese on top of the casserole instead of the American. I like the flavor and texture better.

Cook spaghetti in chicken broth. In a saucepan, saute green pepper in margarine until tender; add flour and stir well. Reduce heat and stir in next 7 ingredients plus 2 cups of American cheese. Cook slowly until cheese is melted and sauce is smooth. Cut chicken into bite-size pieces; add to sauce and stir. Remove from heat. Drain spaghetti and combine with sauce mixture. Season with salt and pepper. Stir well. Spray a 9x13-inch glass dish with nonstick cooking spray. Pour in casserole. Top with remaining cheese and almonds. Bake at 350° for 20 to 30 minutes.

Main Dishes

A mild delicious southwestern flavor as well as a great use for leftover baked ham.

This is a great basic quiche recipe. For variety, use cooked ground beef and green chilies.

Note: If the edge of your pie crust begins to brown too quickly, cover the edge with foil or a "pie shield" (an inexpensive and handy item to have). Also set the pie pan on a metal baking sheet. This helps the bottom brown evenly and keeps the crust from getting soggy.

Ham and Green Chile Quiche

1	unbaked 9-inch, deep-dish pie shell
1½	cups diced ham
⅔	cup green chilies
1½	cups shredded Mexican Blend Cheeses (pre-packaged blend of Monterey Jack, Cheddar, Asadero and Queso Blanco, etc.)
1	cup evaporated milk
½	cup milk
3	large eggs
½	teaspoon seasoned salt
¼	teaspoon fresh ground pepper
dash	cayenne pepper

Preheat oven to 375°. Sprinkle diced ham and green chilies in the bottom of the pie shell. Sprinkle cheese on top. Combine evaporated milk, regular milk, and eggs; beat with a fork or whisk. Make sure ingredients are well combined. Stir in seasonings and pour over ingredients in pie shell. Bake for 45 minutes. Remove from oven and let sit approximately 10 minutes before serving.

Yield: 6-8 servings

Honey Glazed Ham

Main Dishes

1	(14 to 16 pound) old fashion, fully cooked, bone-in ham

Remove hard outer skin from ham, leaving a thin layer of fat. Place ham, fat side up, on a shallow roasting pan. With a sharp knife cut a diamond pattern into the fat. Bake ham for 3 hours at 325°(12 minutes per pound or until internal temperature reaches 130°). Midway through, you may need to cover ham with a foil tent to keep it from getting too brown. Remove from oven, apply glaze, and bake for 30 more minutes.

Glaze:

1⅓	cups firmly packed ˌbrown sugar
⅔	cup sugar
3	teaspoons ground nutmeg
2	teaspoons ground cloves
1	teaspoon ground cinnamon
1	cup honey

Combine sugars and spices; stir until well blended. Using a pastry brush, evenly coat ham with honey. Pat on sugar mixture, thoroughly coating ham.

Note: I find that it helps to put the honey on in small sections then coat with sugar mixture. That way, the honey doesn't run off before you apply the sugar.

Perfect for Easter lunch or dinner! For an unforgettable meal, serve this delicious ham with Baked Cheese Grits (page 126), Marinated Vegetable Salad (page 71), Dell's Creamy Potato Salad (page 70), and Susan's Cheese Rolls (page 41).

Main Dishes

*T*ender and full of flavor, this is another Sunday lunch favorite. Serve with rice or noodles.

Sour Cream Pork Chops

¾	cup flour
1	teaspoon season salt
1	teaspoon fresh ground pepper
½	teaspoon garlic powder
2	tablespoons vegetable oil
6	thick-cut, boneless pork chops
1	large onion, sliced into 6 slices
1	(10½-ounce) can beef bouillon
1	(16-ounce) carton sour cream

Combine flour and seasonings in a plastic bag. Coat pork chops in flour mixture by shaking in bag. In a large skillet, brown pork chops in oil. Remove and place pork chops in a 9x13-inch baking dish that has been sprayed with nonstick cooking spray. Top each chop with onion slice. Blend 2 to 3 tablespoons of flour with drippings in skillet to form a paste. Add bouillon and stir until it thickens. Stir in sour cream. When sauce is well blended pour over the pork chops. Bake covered in a preheated 375° oven for 1 hour then uncover and bake an additional 30 minutes.

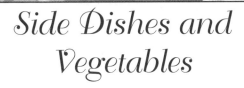

Side Dishes and Vegetables

Food for Thought

In my garden I would plant
five rows of peas:
Preparedness, Promptness, Perseverance,
Politeness, and Prayer.

Next to them I would plant
three rows of squash:
Squash gossip, Squash criticism, and
Squash indifference.

Then I would put in four rows of lettuce:

Let us be faithful.
Let us be unselfish.
Let us be loyal.
Let us love one another.

Author Unknown

Black-Eyed Peas

Naydiene loved fresh black-eyed peas. Now I'm not talking about the dried peas, but fresh peas with plenty of snaps. Every summer she would make sure her son, Dell, planted several rows, so she could freeze enough to enjoy during the winter.

When Naydiene was sick in the hospital, there was a nurse she especially liked from New Zealand. She found out that the nurse, Deanna, had learned to appreciate some of the finer things of Texas life and one of those was black-eyed peas. Naydiene made sure she had Deanna's phone number before she left the hospital, because she wanted to cook her a "mess" of peas. Naydiene was sure Deanna had not tasted fresh black-eyed peas the way she cooked them.

Naydiene did not get the chance to cook those peas. But until the day she died she was always thinking of others and what she could do for them. As her preacher Rodney Plunkett said at her funeral service, "I have been thinking about what Naydiene might be doing in heaven. I thought about the picture in the Bible of going to heaven and there being a great feast. Then it became obvious to me what Naydiene would be doing. She would be cooking, serving, and preparing for the feast."

Baked Rice

3	cups boiling water
3	chicken bouillon cubes
¾	stick butter or margarine
1	cup long grain converted rice
3	tablespoons finely diced onion
3	tablespoons diced green pepper
¼	teaspoon garlic powder
1	teaspoon salt
¾	cup sliced almonds
1	(4-ounce) jar sliced mushrooms

A delicious rice dish that is full of flavor! It is easy to make and is the perfect accompaniment for chicken or beef.

Bring 3 cups of water to a boil, add bouillon cubes; set aside. In a skillet, melt butter, add rice and remaining ingredients, except bouillon. Saute, stirring constantly until rice begins to turn yellow. This will take approximately 5 minutes. Stir in the bouillon. Transfer into a 2-quart, heat resistant, covered glass dish that has been sprayed with nonstick cooking spray. Cover dish with foil then place on lid. This will give you a tighter fit. Bake in a 350° oven for 1 hour. Remove from oven, stir and serve.

Side Dishes

*E*asy to make, this rice is a wonderful side dish. Great with enchiladas or fajitas!

*F*illed with green chiles, sour cream, and cheese this rice dish has a wonderful flavor! It is delicious with grilled chicken or steak. Plus, it is is easy to prepare!

Spanish Rice

⅓   cup vegetable oil
½   cup chopped onion
½   cup chopped green pepper
1   cup uncooked converted rice
¼   teaspoon California-style garlic powder
2   (11.5-ounce) cans V-8 juice
dash of cayenne pepper
salt and fresh ground pepper to taste

Sauté rice, onions, and green pepper until rice begins to turn yellow, approximately 5 minutes. Add garlic powder and V-8 juice. Stir; cover and simmer for 20 minutes. Stir in cayenne, salt, and pepper. Fluff with a fork and serve.

Green Chile Rice

3   cups cooked white rice
2   cups sour cream
salt and pepper to taste
1   (7-ounce) can chopped green chilies
1   tablespoon butter
1½   cups grated Cheddar/Jack cheese blend, divided

To cooked rice, add sour cream, salt, pepper, butter, and green chilies; stir until well mixed. Spray an 8x8-inch glass casserole with nonstick cooking spray. Layer ½ of rice mixture in bottom of casserole, top with ½ of grated cheese. Repeat with remainder of rice and cheese. Bake at 350° for 20 to 30 minutes. Serve hot.

Broccoli and Corn Bake
Aunt Darrell's 1st place recipe

1	pound fresh broccoli or 1 package frozen broccoli
1	(7-ounce) can whole kernel corn
1	(10 ¾-ounce) can cream of mushroom soup, undiluted
½	pound mild Mexican Velveeta
3	tablespoons margarine
1	(6-ounce) package yellow cornbread mix
2	tablespoons dried onion
2	eggs, beaten
1	cup seasoned Italian bread crumbs (optional)

*M*y aunt, Darrell West, was a great cook. She had that special gift of being able to create her own recipes with a little of this and a dash of that. This recipe is one of her originals. Her family liked it so much they suggested she enter it in a local newspaper recipe contest. She won first place!

Prepare broccoli; cook and drain. Drain corn. Heat mushroom soup, cheese, and margarine over low heat until cheese is melted. Combine cornbread mix with dried onion. Stir mushroom soup mixture into cornbread mixture and add beaten eggs. Mix in corn and broccoli; pour into a buttered casserole dish. Sprinkle with bread crumbs and bake for 25 minutes at 400°.

Note: If using an 8x8-inch glass dish, only use half a cup of bread crumbs. This recipe is similar to a cornbread dressing. My family likes it best without the bread crumbs.

125

*M*y son, Logan, could eat an entire pan of these grits! They are his favorite. In fact, they are a family favorite. I often serve them with baked ham. Delicious!

Baked Cheese Grits

6	cups water
1½	cups quick cooking grits (not instant)
2	teaspoons salt
4	cups grated Longhorn Cheddar cheese
⅓	cup butter or margarine
3	teaspoons seasoned salt
¼	teaspoon California-style garlic powder
½	teaspoon paprika
½	teaspoon fresh ground pepper
3	eggs, beaten

Bring 6 cups water to boiling, slowly stir in grits and salt. Reduce heat to medium low and cook for 5 to 7 minutes, or until thickened. Stir occasionally. Stir in grated cheese, butter, and seasonings. Add beaten eggs and stir until well combined. Pour into a 9x13-inch, glass heat-proof dish that has been sprayed with nonstick cooking spray. Bake at 250° for 1½ to 2 hours. Do not rush!

Note: It is best to make cheese grits the day before serving them. That way, they will "firm up" and cut out into nice neat squares. Simply cover with foil and reheat. Cut into squares and serve hot.

Fresh Black-Eyed Peas

2	lbs. fresh black-eyed peas (shelled peas & snaps)
1	stick butter
1	teaspoon sugar
1½	teaspoons salt

After shelling and snapping peas, rinse several times in cool water. Place in a saucepan and add just enough water to cover. Add butter, sugar, and salt. Bring to a boil over medium-high heat. Reduce heat to medium, cover and continue cooking until peas are almost tender. Remove lid and continue cooking until liquid is reduced and peas are tender.

Note: If you are blessed to have a garden, or know someone who does, pick extra peas and freeze them. It's easy to do. Simply rinse shelled peas and snaps well. Prepare a large bowl of ice water with lots of ice; set aside. Place peas in a pot of boiling water. When it reaches a good boil again, boil for 3 minutes. After the 3 minutes, immediately remove the peas and plunge into the ice water. This stops the cooking process. Let the peas sit in the ice water for 3 to 5 minutes. Remove peas with a slotted spoon draining off excess water. Place in zip-top freezer bags. Press out excess air, seal tight, and freeze.

*I*f you have never tasted fresh black-eyed peas you have missed out! I'm not talking about dried or canned. Those are tasteless compared to fresh. You need a combination of fresh shelled peas and the tender snaps. Snaps are the young pods that are too small to shell but "snap" when you break them into pieces. Fresh black-eyed peas will always remind me of Naydiene. They were her favorite!

Side Dishes

*M*y grandmother, Mary West, got this recipe from a friend at her church and shared the recipe with our family. It has been a favorite for years!

Note: Add diced, cooked chicken for a complete one-dish meal!

Broccoli and Rice Casserole

1	small onion, chopped
1½	sticks margarine
1	(10 ¾-ounce) can cream of mushroom soup
1	(8-ounce) jar pasteurized processed cheese spread
½	cup milk
3	cups cooked white rice
2	(10-ounce) packages frozen broccoli spears
	salt and pepper to taste

Sauté onion in margarine until tender. Set aside. Heat soup, cheese, and milk over low heat. Add cooked onions along with margarine. Stir until well combined. Spray a 9x13-inch baking dish with nonstick cooking spray. Place cooked rice in bottom; arrange broccoli spears on top. Pour heated ingredients over top. Bake at 325° for 20 minutes or until sauce is bubbly.

Note: The original recipe called for 2 cups of minute rice. My family likes this dish when I make it with Uncle Ben's Converted White Rice. We also like rice so I use 3 cups of cooked rice. Whichever kind of rice you choose to use this recipe is always delicious!

128

Country Baked Beans

8	slices bacon, diced
½	onion, chopped
1	medium green pepper, chopped
1	(28-ounce) can pork and beans
¾	cup ketchup
½	cup packed brown sugar
¼	cup Woody's Cook-in Sauce

salt and pepper to taste

A summertime favorite, baked beans are the perfect side dish for Dell Burgers (page 108).

Sauté bacon, onion, and green pepper over medium heat until bacon is browned and vegetables are tender. In a large bowl, combine pork and beans with bacon and sautéd vegetables; mix well. Stir in ketchup, brown sugar, and Woody's Cook-in Sauce. Salt and pepper to taste. Pour into a covered baking dish that has been sprayed with nonstick cooking spray. (Note: spray bottom of lid too for easy clean up!) Bake at 425° for 25 minutes; remove lid and bake for an additional 20 minutes or until it begins to brown around the edges.

Woody's Cook-in Sauce is available at your local grocer in the section with other barbeque sauces.

Vegetables

Naydiene's Green Bean and Carrot Casserole

A variation of everyone's favorite green bean casserole, the carrots make this a tasty and colorful side dish.

Time-Saving Tip: Purchase prepackaged baby carrots. They have a great flavor and are already peeled!

¼	cup margarine
½	cup chopped onion
½	cup diced celery
½	cup sliced carrots
2	(14½-ounce) cans French style green beans, drained
1	(10 ¾-ounce) can cream of celery soup
1	small can fried onions
	salt and pepper to taste

Sauté onion, celery, and carrots in margarine until tender. Stir in green beans, soup, and half of the fried onions. Season with salt and pepper to taste. Pour into a covered dish sprayed with nonstick cooking spray. Cook for 30 minutes until bubbly. Uncover; top with the remaining fried onions and bake for 7 more minutes. ˙

Broccoli Sauté

A unique and delicious way to serve broccoli.

2	pounds fresh broccoli
6	slices of bacon
½	cup chopped green onions
¾	cup coarsely chopped pecans

Steam broccoli just until tender. In a large skillet cook bacon until crisp. Remove bacon and crumble. In the same skillet, using bacon drippings, sauté green onions and pecans until onion is tender. Add broccoli and cook for 1 minute, stirring gently. Do not overcook! Transfer to a serving dish and top with crumbled bacon.

Fresh Green Beans

2	lbs. whole fresh green beans (washed and ends removed)
3	slices of uncooked bacon, diced
2	tablespoons butter
1	teaspoon sugar
2	teaspoons salt

Cook diced bacon in saucepan until tender but not crisp. Remove from heat and add whole beans that have been prepared and washed. Pour in just enough water to cover. Add butter, and salt. Place saucepan back on burner and bring to a boil. Reduce heat and cook until tender.

Green Bean Bundles

2	(14.5-ounce) cans whole green beans, drained
8	slices of bacon, cut in half
4	tablespoons butter or margarine
4	tablespoons brown sugar
¼	teaspoon garlic powder
	salt and pepper to taste

Wrap bacon half around 8 to 10 beans to form a bundle. Secure with a toothpick or lay seam side down in a glass baking dish that has been sprayed with nonstick cooking spray. Melt butter in a small saucepan, stir in brown sugar, garlic powder, salt, and pepper. Pour over green bean bundles and bake at 350° for 30 minutes.

Vegetables

Another summer favorite. You can snap the beans into pieces, but we find the whole beans make such an attractive dish. Add toasted sliced almonds for an extra-special touch!

Easy and delicious, a great way to spice up a can of green beans. The presentation makes this a special side dish and it tastes so good that even your kids will eat them!

Vegetables

*R*ich with flavor,
this casserole will
please even those that
think they do not like
broccoli!

Broccoli Casserole

4	cups cooked broccoli spears, chopped
⅓	cup diced onion
4	tablespoons butter
½	cup condensed cream of mushroom soup
¼	cup mayonnaise
¼	teaspoon garlic powder
¼	teaspoon seasoned salt
	fresh ground pepper to taste

Steam broccoli spears until tender; chop into bite size pieces. Sauté onion in butter until tender. Combine broccoli, sautéd onions, and remaining ingredients; mix well. Pour into a casserole dish and add topping.

Topping:

½	cup crushed round buttery crackers
1	tablespoon butter, melted

Stir crushed crackers in melted butter and sprinkle on top of casserole. Bake in a preheated 350° oven for 20 to 25 minutes.

Glazed Carrots

1	(2-pound) package peeled baby carrots
2	tablespoons sugar
2	teaspoons cornstarch
½	teaspoon salt
½	cup orange juice
2	tablespoons butter

The diagonal cut and delicious glaze make this carrot dish especially attractive!

Cut carrots diagonally into ¼-inch slices. Cook carrots in boiling water until tender (about 10 minutes); drain. Set carrots aside but keep warm. Combine sugar, cornstarch, and salt in a small saucepan; slowly stir in orange juice. Bring to a boil and boil one minute, stirring constantly. Remove from heat, stir in butter. Pour glaze over cooked carrots, toss to coat.

Yield: 10 to 12 servings

Quick Buttered Carrots

Easy to make! For variety stir in ½ cup frozen English peas. Continue cooking until peas are warm.

2	cups small baby carrots
2	tablespoons butter
½	cup water
	salt and pepper to taste

Place carrots, butter, and water in a saucepan. Bring to a boil. Cover and reduce heat. Simmer until tender; approximately 20 minutes. Season with salt and pepper to taste.

Time-Saving Tip: Buy packages of peeled baby carrots at your local grocer.

Vegetables

A West Texas tradition! Fried okra is always a favorite. The light cornmeal coating adds to the flavor, yet is not so heavy that you can't taste the okra. There is no need to dip the okra or potatoes in egg. I find that process messy plus too much batter hides the great flavor of the okra!

*N*aydiene discovered that cooking whole okra pods in the microwave is quick, easy, and delicious! Yes, the okra still has it's slimy texture even cooked this way, but to many Southerners that is part of it's charm! My children even like okra prepared this way.

Fried Okra & Potatoes

12	medium-size okra pods, sliced
1	medium-size baking potato, peeled and cubed
1	cup cornmeal
½	cup all-purpose flour
salt to taste	

Wash okra pods and trim off both ends. Leaving the okra a little damp will help the cornmeal stick to it later. Slice into ½ inch slices. Peel and cube potatoes. Combine cornmeal and flour in a plastic zip-top bag. If desired, sprinkle okra and potatoes with salt. Place a handful of okra slices and potato cubes into cornmeal mixture; shake until coated. Fry in vegetable oil using a deep fryer or cast-iron skillet until golden brown. Drain on paper towels and serve.

Naydiene's Okra

24	whole young okra pods (approximately 2 inches in length)
2	tablespoons of butter or margarine
salt and pepper to taste	

Wash okra and trim stem. Leave okra damp and place whole pods in a single layer in a microwave-safe dish. Dot with butter. Cover with plastic wrap and microwave for 6 to 10 minutes or until okra is tender. Salt and pepper to taste.

Karen's Sweet Potato Casserole

5	large sweet potatoes, peeled and cut into ¾-inch slices
⅓	cup packed brown sugar, divided
½	teaspoon salt, divided
4	tablespoons margarine, divided into ¼-inch slices
¾	cup coarsely chopped pecans

Preheat oven to 400°. Spray a 9x13-inch baking dish with nonstick cooking spray. Arrange half of the sweet potato slices in dish. Sprinkle with half of the brown sugar, salt, and dot with half of the margarine. Layer remaining potatoes, brown sugar, salt, and margarine. Cover with foil and bake for 30 minutes. Remove foil, sprinkle on pecans, and bake uncovered an additional 30 minutes or until potatoes are tender.

Note: To keep potatoes from drying out, baste with the syrup that forms in the bottom of the dish several times while cooking.

A holiday favorite my sister, Karen, brings this wonderful dish.

Note: To keep sweet potatoes from turning dark, let slices sit for 5 minutes in two cups of cold water to which 1 ½ tablespoons of lemon juice have been added. Drain well and blot with paper towels.

Vegetables

*M*y husband, Dell, did not really like squash until he tasted this casserole! The recipe came from his aunt, Mack Cannon. The stuffing mix adds lots of flavor and the casserole is very easy to make. It also freezes well.

Note: Approximately 6 to 8 medium squash will equal two pounds. Use fresh yellow summer squash. You do not need to peel the squash. Just cut off both ends and slice.

Aunt Mack's Squash Casserole

1 ½   lbs. yellow squash, sliced
       and cooked until tender
1   stick margarine, melted
1   (6-ounce) box Stove Top
       cornbread stuffing mix
1   (8-ounce) carton sour cream
1   (10 ¾-ounce) can cream of
       chicken soup, undiluted
       salt and pepper to taste

Cook squash until tender. (Note: you can steam it or cook in boiling water). Drain well. Combine melted margarine with stuffing mix; stir until well blended. Set aside. In a large bowl, combine cooked squash, sour cream, and soup; stir until well mixed. Stir in half of the stuffing mix. Salt and pepper to taste. Pour in a 9x13-inch baking dish that has been sprayed with nonstick cooking spray. Top with remaining stuffing mix. Bake at 350° for about 30 minutes or until it is bubbly and lightly browned on the top.

Grandmother's Baked Squash

2	pounds yellow squash, sliced
½	onion, chopped
¼	cup sour cream
	salt and pepper to taste

Boil squash and onion together until tender. Drain well. Mash squash with potato masher; drain again. Stir in sour cream; season to taste. Place in a 1½-quart covered casserole dish that has been sprayed with nonstick cooking spray. Bake at 350° for 20 minutes; uncover and bake 10 more minutes

*A*n old-fashioned favorite, Naydiene said this was the way her mother cooked squash. It is simple to make and has a wonderful flavor.

Grilled Squash & Onions

4	yellow squash, sliced
1	Vidalia or 1015 onion, sliced
1	green pepper, cut into strips
6	tablespoons butter
	seasoned salt and fresh ground pepper to taste

Spray a large sheet of heavy-duty foil with nonstick cooking spray. Layer sliced squash, sliced onion, and strips of green pepper. Sprinkle each layer with seasoned salt and fresh ground pepper. Dot with butter. Continue layering until you have used all of the vegetables. Seal edges of foil. Place on grill. (Note: It is best to cook this on indirect heat. We cook this on the upper rack of our grill.) Cook for about 20 minutes.

*W*e love to grill during the summer. This is an easy and delicious way to cook squash.

Note: Vidalia and 1015 onions are available during the summer. Any type of sweet onion will work.

Variation: Add fresh tomatoes and basil.

Vegetables

Another Sunday lunch favorite! My family loves this dish.

Note: Do not defrost the hash browns. If they are thawed this casserole becomes too mushy. Also if you are out of cornflakes it is still good even without the topping.

Hash Brown Casserole

1	(32-ounce) package frozen hash brown potatoes
1	(10 ¾-ounce) can cream of chicken soup
1	(8-ounce) carton sour cream
¾	stick margarine, melted
2	cups grated Cheddar cheese
1	teaspoon salt
¼	teaspoon pepper
½	cup finely chopped onion or 1 teaspoon onion powder

Topping:

2	cups crushed corn flakes
2	tablespoons margarine, melted

Break apart frozen hash browns and place in a large bowl. In another bowl, combine soup, sour cream, and melted margarine; stir until well blended. Add grated cheese; stir well. Stir in salt, pepper, and onion. Pour mixture over frozen hash browns and stir until thoroughly mixed. Spray a 9x13-inch glass dish with nonstick cooking spray. Pour in casserole. Prepare topping by combining crushed cornflakes with 2 tablespoons melted margarine; toss to coat. Sprinkle on top of casserole. Bake at 350° for 45 minutes.

Festive Potato Casserole

3	pounds baking potatoes, peeled and cut into chunks
½	cup butter
2	(3-ounce) packages cream cheese, softened
1	cup grated Cheddar cheese
¾	cup finely diced green pepper
½	cup finely diced green onion
1	(4-ounce) jar diced pimento, drained
½	cup fresh grated Parmesan cheese
½	cup milk
2	teaspoons salt

As attractive as it is delicious, this potato casserole is a favorite.

Note: You can simply whip the potatoes with a whisk or use an electric mixer.

Cover potatoes with water and boil until tender (test with fork); drain and mash. Add butter and cream cheese; whip until smooth and creamy. Stir in Cheddar cheese, green pepper, pimento, Parmesan, milk and salt; blend well. Spoon mixture into a lightly greased, round, 2-quart glass casserole dish. Bake uncovered at 350° for 25 minutes. Top with additional grated Cheddar cheese; bake an additional 5 minutes or until cheese melts and casserole is heated throughout.

Yield: 8 servings

Vegetables

A classic family favorite! My mom has to double this recipe when all of the grandkids come because they love scalloped potatoes! The perfect side dish to go with Mom's Meat Loaf (page 99) or Mom's Brisket (page 95). Yum!

Another favorite "comfort food"! There is nothing like homemade mashed potatoes to feed your body and warm your soul! Serve with Mom's Meat Loaf (page 99).

Scalloped Potatoes

5	baking potatoes, peeled and thinly sliced
3	tablespoons flour
1	stick butter or margarine
1 to 2	cups warm milk
½	cup grated Cheddar cheese

In a lightly greased, 2-quart casserole dish, place a layer of potato slices. Sprinkle potatoes with 1 tablespoon of flour. Sprinkle layer with salt and pepper; dot with butter. Continue layering potatoes in this manner. Pour in enough milk to just cover potatoes. Bake in a 350° oven for approximately 1 hour or until potatoes are tender. Top with grated Cheddar cheese; return to oven for 5 minutes or until cheese melts.

Mashed Potatoes

3 to 4	baking potatoes, peeled and cut into chunks
1	stick butter
½	cup warm milk
	salt and fresh ground pepper

Cook potatoes in boiling salted water until tender. (Check with a fork.) Drain well. Add butter and mash with potato masher. Stir in milk and mix with potato masher or electric mixer. Season with salt and pepper. Whip until smooth and creamy. (Note: You can whip them with the potato masher or a whisk, you do not have to use a mixer.)

Desserts

Home is...

where you can be silent
and still be heard.

where you can ask and
find out who you are.

where people laugh with
you about yourself.

where sorrow is divided
and joy multiplied.

Author Unknown

Naydiene's Recipe Box

After Naydiene passed away, we had the difficult task of parting with Dell's childhood home and sifting through the things left behind. I remember picking up her recipe box, the one she tole painted to match her canister set, the one that always sat on her kitchen counter, the one that held her handwritten recipe cards. I could still see her thumbing through it, looking for that favorite recipe. As I picked it up I thought, "I wish this held the secret to her great cooking, but so much of it was in her head! Oh well, at least it's filled with great recipes and many of Dell's favorites!"

As we continued sorting through the memories and mementos collected through the years, I ran across another recipe box. Now this box was a funny color, an old tin box crudely painted. I thought, "Why in the world did she save this! The painting is so bad I would have thrown this away." I turned it over and there were her initials and the year, 1966. It was one of the first things she ever painted. Then I realized, when I first met her in 1981 she had been painting for 15 years. No wonder her tole painting was beautiful, she'd had a lot of practice!

At that point, I had another revelation. I had judged myself in the same way by comparing a new bride, who was just learning to be a wife, to a woman who had been a wife for over 35 years! I picked up the crudely painted recipe box, realizing I had just learned another lesson, a lesson in patience and perseverance. I smiled with the knowledge that Naydiene was continuing to teach me through the legacy she left behind. Naydiene had a lot of pretty things, but I think her old recipe box is my favorite.

Fresh Apple Cake
Aunt Darrell's original recipe

3	cups flour
½	teaspoon ground cloves
½	teaspoon nutmeg
1	teaspoon cinnamon
1	teaspoon salt
½	teaspoon soda
2	cups sugar
3	eggs, slightly beaten
1½	cups vegetable oil
1	teaspoon vanilla
3	cups peeled, diced apples
1	large carrot, grated
1	cup chopped pecans

Sift together flour, spices, salt, and soda. Combine in a bowl with sugar. By hand, stir in eggs, oil, and vanilla. Add apples, grated carrot, and pecans, stirring until well mixed. Batter will be very thick. Pour into greased and floured bundt pan or three loaf pans. Bake in preheated 350° oven for 1 hour. Remove from oven and cool. When cool, transfer to serving plate and cover with icing. Note: The icing is optional. We like this cake just as well without icing.

For icing combine the following:

1	(1-pound) box powdered sugar
½	stick margarine, melted
1	teaspoon vanilla

enough apple juice to make the right spreading consistency

This fresh apple cake is an original recipe of my Aunt Darrell's. She was a wonderful cook and took great delight in coming up with new and different recipes. Throughout this cook book, there are several of her recipes. Each one is special, just like she was.

Note: Use a good baking apple like a Jonagold or Granny Smith.

Note: This cake freezes well and keeps in the refrigerator for up to two weeks.

143

Cakes

A delicious pound cake! West Texans love apricots and this cake is always a favorite.

Helpful Hint: To test whether a bundt cake is done, use a long wooden skewer (available at your local grocer). This works much better than a toothpick when testing deep cakes like a bundt or pound cake.

Note: This cake freezes well.

Apricot Pound Cake

1	box pound cake mix
1	(3-ounce) box lemon jello
½	cup salad oil
⅔	cup apricot nectar
2	teaspoons lemon extract
5	eggs

Combine all ingredients except eggs. Add eggs one at a time and beat well after adding each egg. Pour batter in a greased and floured bundt cake pan and bake in a 350° oven for 40 minutes. Cool. Turn cake out of pan and spoon glaze over cake.

Glaze:

½	cup apricot nectar
½	cup sugar

In a sauce pan, combine sugar and apricot nectar. Over medium heat, stir mixture until sugar is melted. Do not boil. Spoon glaze over cake.

Chocolate Rum Cake

1	cup finely chopped pecans
1	box Duncan Hines yellow cake mix
1	(6-ounce) package instant chocolate pudding
½	cup rum
¾	cup water
¾	cup vegetable oil
4	eggs

I have more requests for this recipe than any of my other cake recipes. It is so easy to make and always moist and delicious!

Grease a bundt pan. Place chopped nuts in bottom of pan. Combine cake mix, pudding mix, rum, water, oil, and eggs in mixing bowl. Mix 2 minutes at medium speed. Pour into bundt pan. Bake in a 325° oven for approximately 1 hour. Cake is ready when top springs back when lightly touched. Remove cake from oven and leave in pan. Prepare glaze.

For a great teacher or co-worker gift, use small bundt pans and make individual mini rum cakes.

Note: If you would like, you can substitute rum flavoring for the rum.

Glaze:

½	cup butter
1	cup brown sugar
¼	cup rum
¼	cup water

Boil butter, brown sugar, rum, and water for 2 minutes. Pour over top of cake while it is still in the pan. Cool cake for 30 minutes then turn out onto serving plate. Delicious!

Cakes

*M*om always made cakes from scratch and this was one of my favorites growing up. Delicious when iced with Mom's White Icing!

Note: Grease your cake pans well with vegetable shortening. Simply use a paper towel to spread it evenly then coat the pans with flour.

Helpful Hint: Freeze cake layers before icing them. This helps to keep the cake crumbs from getting into the icing and gives you a firmer surface to spread the icing on.

Mom's Chocolate Cake

2	eggs, separated
1½	cups sugar, divided
1½	cups sifted flour
¾	teaspoon soda
¾	teaspoon salt
⅓	cup cocoa
⅓	cup Wesson oil
1	cup buttermilk

Beat egg whites until fluffy, add ½ cup sugar. In a large mixing bowl combine remaining cup of sugar, flour, soda, salt, and cocoa. Add oil and ½ of milk, beat well. Add egg yolks and other ½ of milk. Beat another minute. Fold in egg whites. Pour batter into two, greased and floured 9-inch cake pans. Bake in a 350° oven for 25 to 30 minutes.

Mom's White Icing

1	stick margarine or butter, softened
2-3	tablespoons milk
1	(1-pound) box powdered sugar
½	teaspoon vanilla

Cream butter, gradually add powdered sugar, alternating with milk. Add vanilla. Beat until creamy.

Chocolate Chip Pound Cake

1	box yellow or white cake mix
1	(3-ounce) box instant vanilla pudding
1	(3-ounce) box instant chocolate pudding
4	eggs
½	cup oil
1½	cups water
1	cup chopped pecans
1	cup semi-sweet mini chocolate chips

I love bundt cakes because they are easy to make and they are usually so rich that they do not require icing. This one is especially good!

Combine first 6 ingredients in mixing bowl. Beat for 3 minutes at medium speed. Stir in pecans and chocolate chips. Bake in greased and floured bundt pan at 350° for 1 hour to 1 hour 15 minutes. Let cake cool 20 minutes before removing from pan.

Note: Lightly coat pecans with flour so they will not sink to the bottom of the cake.

Golden Chocolate Chip Cake

Made with a yellow cake mix and vanilla pudding, this bundt cake is moist and delicious. Filled with chocolate chips and pecans, it is rich and does not need icing.

Note: Remember to coat the chocolate chips and the pecans with one tablespoon of flour. This will keep them from sinking to the bottom of the pan.

1	box yellow cake mix
1	(6-ounce) box instant vanilla pudding
3	eggs
¾	cup vegetable oil
1	(8-ounce) carton sour cream
¾	cup water
¾	cup chopped pecans
1	(12-ounce) package of miniature semi-sweet chocolate chips

Combine cake mix, pudding, eggs, oil, sour cream, and water in mixing bowl. Beat 4 minutes. Stir in pecans and chocolate chips. Bake in greased and floured bundt pan at 300° for 50 to 55 minutes. Cool in pan for 20 minutes before turning out onto a plate.

Cream Cheese Pound Cake

2	sticks margarine
1	stick butter
3	cups sugar
1	(8-ounce) package cream cheese
6	large eggs, separated
1½	teaspoons vanilla
¼	teaspoon salt
3	cups sifted cake flour

Cream margarine, butter and sugar; add cream cheese. Beat well. Add egg yolks, one at a time, beating well after each yolk. Add vanilla and salt. Blend in sifted flour. Gently fold in beaten egg whites with a spoon. Bake at 325° for 1 hour in a greased and floured bundt pan. Let cool in pan for 15 to 20 minutes before removing.

Cream Cheese Icing

1	(3-ounce) package cream cheese, softened
3	tablespoons margarine
1	teaspoon vanilla
2	cups powdered sugar
pinch	of salt
½	cup chopped, toasted pecans

Cream together cream cheese, margarine, vanilla, and powdered sugar. Add salt and toasted pecans.

This wonderfully rich cake is one of my favorites! It is delicious without icing, but for an extra special taste, frost it with cream cheese icing. Like many pound cakes, it improves with age, so make it 2 to 3 days before serving.

Note: Toasting the pecans enhances their flavor. To toast spread the pecans on a baking sheet with sides and cook at 350° for 10 to 15 minutes stirring occasionally. Let them cool before stirring into the icing.

Cakes

*I*f you like coconut
you will love this pound
cake! It is moist and
delicious!

Serving Suggestion:
Top each slice with
fresh strawberries
and whipped cream.

Coconut Pound Cake

2	sticks margarine or butter
½	cup shortening
3	cups sugar
6	eggs
3	cups flour
1	cup milk
1	teaspoon almond flavoring
1	teaspoon coconut flavoring
¼	teaspoon salt
1 ½	cup frozen coconut

Cream margarine, shortening, and sugar. Add eggs one at a time. Beat well. Alternately adding flour and milk. Add flavorings and salt; beat well. Stir in coconut. Pour into a greased and floured bundt pan. Start in a cold oven. Set oven temperature to 350°. Bake 1 hour and 15 minutes or until cake tester comes out clean.

Créme De Menthe Cake

1	box regular white cake mix (not pudding type)
2	egg whites
1	cup plus 3 tablespoons water
¼	cup créme de menthe, divided
1	(16-ounce) can chocolate fudge icing
1	(8-ounce) carton frozen whipped topping, thawed

Combine cake mix, egg whites, water, and 2 tablespoons créme de menthe. Beat 2 minutes on high speed. Reduce to low and beat another minute. Pour into greased and floured 9x13-inch cake pan. Bake in a preheated 350° oven for 25 minutes or until a toothpick comes out clean. Let cake cool completely in pan. Spread fudge icing over cake. Combine whipped topping with 2 tablespoons créme de menthe. Spread over fudge icing. Cover and chill at least 2 hours.

Chocolate Leaves

6 to 8	lemon leaves with stems
2	ounces of semi-sweet chocolate

Wash and dry well. Melt chocolate. Using a small spatula, coat the underside of the leaves. Do not let it run over the edges. Place coated leaves on waxed paper, chocolate side up. Chill until set. To remove leaf simply grab stem and gently peel off the leaf. Chill chocolate leaves until ready to use.

The combination of chocolate and mint flavor makes this cake cool and delicious!

Serving Suggestion: This cake is best when it is chilled throughout. I recommend chilling it overnight. To serve, cut into squares and top with chocolate leaves if desired.

Note: Use a shiny non-poisonous leaf. Also you can melt chocolate in the microwave. Heat at 50% power for 1 minute and stir until smooth and creamy.

Cakes	

Grandmother's German Chocolate Cake

*A*t our West Family gatherings, we always had a variety of desserts and this was one of my favorites. My Grandmother West always made this cake, it was her favorite too!

1	(4-ounce) package German sweet chocolate
½	cup water
2	cups sifted flour
1	teaspoon baking soda
¼	teaspoon salt
1	cup margarine or butter
2	cups sugar
4	eggs, separated
1	teaspoon vanilla
1	cup buttermilk

Preheat oven to 350°. Line bottom of three 9-inch cake pans with wax paper. Place chocolate and water in microwave safe bowl. Microwave on high for 1 minute. Stir. Microwave another minute then stir until chocolate is completely melted. Set aside. Combine flour, soda, and salt; set aside. In a mixing bowl, cream margarine and sugar until light and fluffy. Add egg yolks, 1 at a time, beating after each addition. Stir in chocolate mixture and vanilla. Add flour mixture alternately with butter-milk. Beat until smooth. Beat egg whites until stiff. Gently fold into batter. Pour into prepared pans. Bake 30 minutes or until cake springs back when lightly touched. Remove from oven and immediately run metal spatula or knife around sides of pan. Cool 15 minutes then remove from pan and peel off wax paper. Place on wire racks and cool completely. When cool, spread with Coconut-Pecan Frosting (page 153).

Coconut Pecan Frosting

1	(12-ounce) can evaporated milk
1 ½	cups sugar
1 ½	sticks margarine or butter
4	egg yolks, slightly beaten
1½	teaspoons vanilla
2 ⅔	cups angel flake coconut
1 ½	cups chopped pecans

*T*his icing provides the perfect finish to Grandmother's German Chocolate Cake.

Combine milk, sugar, margarine, egg yolks, and vanilla in large saucepan. Cook over medium heat about 12 minutes, stirring until thick and golden brown. Remove from heat. Stir in coconut and pecans. Beat until cool. Spread between cake layers and on top, but not on side of cake.

Fresh Coconut Cake

1	box yellow cake mix

Prepare according to package directions. Bake in 2 greased and floured 8-inch cake pans for 30 to 35 minutes. Slice each layer in half, making 4 layers.

Filling:

2	cups sugar
2	cups sour cream
2	cups grated fresh coconut or flake coconut

Combine sugar, sour cream, and coconut. Spread between layers on top and sides of cake. Garnish top with more coconut. Store in refrigerator for 3 to 4 days <u>before</u> serving.

*A*n old-fashioned family favorite, this cake does require advance preparation, but it is worth it! This cake reminds me of my grandmothers. I can remember each of them having this cake in the refrigerator ready to serve at a special family gathering.

153

Cakes

My sister, Karen, makes this delicious cheesecake for our family holidays. It is the best cheesecake, so creamy! Karen likes to top it with fresh fruit. She often uses fresh blueberries and straw-berries for the 4th of July and fresh kiwi and strawberries layered on top for Christmas. If you are in a hurry, chilled canned cherry pie filling is also good.

Note: After adding the sour cream, the springform pan will be very full and heavy. Placing it on a cookie sheet makes it easier to lift and place back in the oven.

Karen's Creamy Cheesecake

Crust:

16	graham crackers, crushed
2	tablespoons sugar
6	tablespoons butter, melted
1½	teaspoons cinnamon

Mix all ingredients and press into bottom of a springform pan. Refrigerate until ready to fill.

3	(8-ounce) packages cream cheese, softened
3	eggs
1	cup sugar
1½	pints sour cream
3	tablespoons sugar

Beat cream cheese until creamy. In another bowl, beat eggs until fluffy. Add sugar gradually and beat until smooth and a pale yellow color (beat about 10 minutes). Do not rush this step, be patient and beat for the full 10 minutes or your cheese cake will be lumpy. Combine cream cheese and egg mixture; mix thoroughly. Pour into crust and bake 20 minutes at 375°. Take out of oven and place pan on a cookie sheet. Turn oven temperature up to 500°. Thoroughly mix sour cream with 3 tablespoons sugar and pour on cheesecake. Return to oven for 5 minutes. Remove from oven and cool. Chill completely before serving. It is best if made the day before and allowed to chill overnight. Serve with your favorite topping.

Italian Cream Cake

2	cups sugar
1	stick margarine or butter, softened
½	cup shortening
5	eggs, separated
2	cups flour
1	teaspoon soda
1	cup buttermilk
1	cup angel flake coconut
1	cup chopped pecans

Rich and delicious, filled with pecans and coconut, and layered with creamy cream cheese frosting, this is a classic favorite!

Cream sugar, margarine, and shortening. Add yolks, one at a time beating after each addition. Add sifted dry ingredients, alternating with buttermilk. Add coconut. Beat egg whites until stiff and fold in. Add pecans and gently fold in. Pour into 3 greased and floured 8-inch cake pans. Bake in a preheated 350° oven for 25 minutes. Cool cake layers and ice with cream cheese icing.

Icing:

1	stick margarine or butter, softened
1	(8-ounce) package cream cheese, softened
1½	teaspoons vanilla
1	(1-pound) box powdered sugar, sifted
pinch	salt (optional)
1	cup toasted pecans, chopped

Note: Toasting the pecans enhances their flavor. See page 149 for directions on toasting pecans.

Cream margarine, cream cheese, and vanilla. Add powdered sugar and salt. Blend well. Stir in pecans. Spread frosting between layers, on sides and on top.

Cakes

*N*aydiene often made this cake during the holidays. She was always busy around Christmas baking cakes as gifts to her friends and in preparation for holiday guests. This cake filled with fruit, coconut, and pecans, is moist and delicious!

Hummingbird Cake

1½	cups oil
2	cups sugar
3	eggs
1	teaspoon vanilla
3	cups flour
1	teaspoon soda
1	teaspoon cinnamon
1	(15-ounce) can crushed pineapple in heavy syrup
2	cups bananas, diced
1	cup pecans, chopped
1	cup coconut

Combine oil, sugar, eggs, and vanilla. Stir mixture thoroughly, but do not use a mixer. Add dry sifted ingredients; mix well. Blend in fruit and nuts. Pour into a greased and floured tube pan and bake in a preheated 325° oven for 1½ hours. Cool completely before trying to remove from pan.

Icing:

2	(8-ounce) packages cream cheese, softened
1	cup butter, softened
2	(1-pound) boxes powdered sugar
2	teaspoons vanilla

Cream together ingredients then mix in enough milk to make mixture spreadable. Spread icing on cooled cake.

Mississippi Mud Cake

1	cup margarine
2	cups sugar
4	eggs
1½	cups flour
¼	teaspoon salt
⅓	cup cocoa
3	teaspoons vanilla
1	cup chopped pecans
1	(7-ounce) jar marshmallow creme

Cream margarine and sugar. Add eggs one at a time; mixing after each addition. Add flour, cocoa, and salt. Blend well. Stir in vanilla and pecans. Pour in a greased and floured 9x13-inch pan. Bake at 325° for 25 to 30 minutes or until toothpick comes out clean. Pour marshmallow creme over hot cake. Let cake and marshmallow creme layer cool, then spread on icing.

Icing:

⅓	cup cocoa
⅔	stick margarine
¼	cup milk
1	(1-pound) box powdered sugar
½	cup chopped pecans

Place cocoa, margarine, milk, and vanilla in top of double boiler. Cook until margarine is melted and ingredients combine; stir occasionally. Stir in powdered sugar and nuts. Stir until well mixed. Pour over cake.

A rich chocolate cake filled with pecans and marshmallow creme! This cake is a family favorite, especially among those of us who love chocolate!

Note: To soften the marshmallow creme so it will pour, take off lid and microwave on high for 30 to 45 seconds.

This recipe came from my cousin, Rosemary West. We have enjoyed it for years.

Cakes

*M*y brother, Glenn, loves this cake and so does the rest of our family! The cake is filled with spices and the rich icing adds the perfect finishing touch.

For a change of pace, prepare the cake in a bundt pan and pour the icing (like a glaze) over the cake.

Mom's Spice Cake

2	cups sifted flour
1	cup sugar
1	teaspoon baking powder
1	teaspoon salt
¾	teaspoon soda
¾	teaspoon ground cloves
¾	teaspoon ground cinnamon
⅔	cup shortening
¾	cup brown sugar
1	cup buttermilk
3	eggs

Sift together first 7 ingredients. Add shortening, brown sugar and buttermilk; mix until flour is moistened. Beat 2 minutes at medium speed. Add eggs, beat 2 minutes more. Bake in 2 greased and lightly floured 9-inch cake pans at 350° for 30 to 35 minutes. Cool 10 minutes then remove from pans. Cool completely on cake rack.

Icing:

2	cups brown sugar, packed
½	cup milk
½	cup butter or margarine
¼	teaspoon salt
1	teaspoon vanilla

Mix all ingredients except vanilla in a saucepan. Place over low heat and bring slowly to a boil, stirring constantly. Boil hard 2 minutes then remove from heat and beat until lukewarm. Add vanilla and beat with mixer until thick enough to spread. (It will take awhile, just be patient because the end result is worth the effort! Delicious!)

Aunt Darrell's
Twenty-Two Minute Cake

2	cups sugar
2	cups flour
1	cup water
½	cup shortening
1	stick margarine
3½	tablespoons cocoa
½	cup buttermilk
2	eggs
1	teaspoon soda
1	teaspoon vanilla

Do not use mixer! Combine sugar and flour in a large bowl. In a small saucepan, combine water, shortening, margarine, and cocoa. Bring to a boil. Pour over flour-sugar mixture. Combine milk, eggs, soda, and vanilla. Add to other mixture and stir until blended. Pour into a greased and floured 12x18-inch pan. Bake for 22 minutes at 400°. When cake has cooled 10 minutes cover with icing.

Icing:

1	stick margarine
3½	tablespoons cocoa
⅓	cup milk
1	(1-pound) box powdered sugar
1	cup chopped pecans

In a saucepan, combine margarine, cocoa, and milk. Bring to a boil. Add powdered sugar and chopped pecans. Pour over <u>hot</u> cake.

*M*any cooks, especially in West Texas, have made this cake for years. Maybe it is because my Aunt Darrell shared her recipe in the local newspaper the Lubbock Avalanche-Journal, back in 1966. Aunt Darrell was an accomplished artist and a great cook. But the thing I admired most about her was her love for life and her ability to make everyone she met feel special! Her daughters, Donna and Danna, think this recipe originally belonged to Darrell's mother, Mildred Barney.

Cakes

*T*his basic white cake has been used for many special occasions over the years. Everyone has a favorite icing and of course Mom always made our favorite on our birthdays!

*A*lways a favorite, chocolate icing makes a basic white cake taste extra special!

Basic White Cake

2	cups sifted flour
3½	teaspoons baking powder
1⅓	cups sugar
1	teaspoon salt
½	cup shortening
1	cup milk, divided
½	cup egg whites
1	teaspoon vanilla

Sift together flour, baking powder, sugar, and salt. Add shortening and ¾ cup milk; beat for 2 minutes or until mixture is well blended. Add ¼ cup milk, unbeaten egg whites, and vanilla. Beat for 2 minutes. Pour into 2 well greased and floured 8-inch cake pans. Bake in a 350° oven for 25 to 30 minutes.

Chocolate Icing

½	cup shortening
½	cup butter
1	pound box powdered sugar
3	ounces unsweetened chocolate, melted
3	tablespoons milk
1	teaspoon vanilla

Cream shortening and butter. Gradually add powdered sugar and melted chocolate alternating with milk. Stir in vanilla. Blend on medium speed until creamy.

Daddy's Favorite Pineapple Cake

Bake Mom's Basic White Cake or any white layer cake then ice with pineapple icing.

Icing:

1	**(15-ounce) can crushed pineapple with juice**
⅔	**cup sugar**
½	**cup flour**
⅓	**cup lemon juice**
½	**teaspoon pineapple flavoring**

Combine all ingredients in a saucepan and cook until thick, stirring constantly. Cool.

As the title says, this is my Dad's all-time favorite cake. And if you like pineapple, it will become one of your favorites too!

Seven Minute Frosting

Another icing recipe that can be used with Mom's Basic White Cake to make a completely different cake.

2	**egg whites**
1½	**cups sugar**
1½	**teaspoons light corn syrup**
¼	**teaspoon cream of tartar**
⅓	**cup cold water**
dash	**of salt**
½	**teaspoon vanilla**
1	**cup coconut**

Combine all ingredients except vanilla and coconut in a double boiler stirring until blended. Place mixture over boiling water. Using an electric hand mixer, beat constantly on high speed for 7 minutes or until icing peaks. Remove from heat. Add vanilla. Ice cake and sprinkle with coconut.

I love this icing, especially on Mom's white cake. I often requested it for my birthday cake. Not only does it make a pretty cake it is also delicious!

For variety, tint the white cake pink.

161

Cakes

*A*n old-fashioned
favorite, this cake is
more like a spice cake.
So if you are thinking...
"I don't like prunes so I
won't like this cake," you
ought to try it because
you might be surprised.
Moist and delicious it is
good without icing, but
you can add the glaze if
you like.

Prune Cake

1	cup vegetable oil
2	cups sugar
3	eggs
2	cups flour, sifted
1	teaspoon baking soda
1	teaspoon nutmeg
1	teaspoon cinnamon
1	teaspoon salt
¼	teaspoon allspice
1	cup buttermilk
1	teaspoon vanilla
1	(7 ½-ounce) jar junior baby food prunes
1	cup finely chopped pecans

Mix vegetable oil and sugar together. Add eggs, beating after each addition. Sift together flour, soda, nutmeg, cinnamon, allspice, and salt. Gradually add dry ingredients alternating with buttermilk. Blend in vanilla and prunes. Mix well. Stir in pecans. Pour into a greased and floured tube pan. Bake in a 325° oven for 1 hour or until toothpick comes out clean. Cool in pan 10 to 15 minutes. Remove from pan and brush with glaze while still warm.

Glaze:

1	cup powdered sugar
2	tablespoons butter, softened
3	tablespoons milk
½	teaspoon vanilla

Combine all ingredients stirring until smooth. Brush onto warm cake.

My Favorite Chocolate Pie

Pies

1	cup sugar
⅓	cup cocoa
½	cup flour
½	teaspoon salt
2	cups milk
3	egg yolks, beaten
1	teaspoon vanilla
1	teaspoon butter

In a large saucepan or skillet, combine sugar, cocoa, flour, and salt. In a small bowl, combine milk and egg yolks, stir with a fork until blended. Gradually add milk mixture to dry ingredients, stirring until smooth. Cook over medium heat, stirring constantly, until mixture thickens and is bubbly. Set off of heat, add vanilla and butter. When mixture has cooled slightly, pour into baked pie crust. Top with meringue.

Meringue:

3	egg whites
6	tablespoons sugar
¼	teaspoon cream of tartar

Beat egg whites, gradually adding sugar and cream of tartar. Continue beating until egg whites form stiff peaks. Top pie with meringue and swirl with a spoon for an attractive look. Note: For the best results, make sure your custard has cooled to room temperature and that you spread meringue to the edges of the crust (this will help keep your pie from weeping). Brown in a 350° oven for 10 to 15 minutes or until lightly browned. Cool completely before serving.

This is my absolute favorite! I have such fond childhood memories associated with chocolate pie. My grandfather "Pa" always told a story about when I was a little girl. Granny made a chocolate pie while I was visiting and the next night after supper, I wanted a piece for dessert, but Granny said there was only a very small piece left. As the story goes, I looked at Pa and said, "If you hadn't eaten such a big piece yesterday, there would be plenty left!" Pa told this story over and over again always laughing as he told it. That memory and the taste of homemade chocolate pie always makes me think of him!

163

Pies

My mom makes the best pie crust I have ever tasted! When I was growing up she would take the leftover dough and pat it into small cookie size pieces. She would then sprinkle them with cinnamon and sugar and bake them until they were golden brown. This was a special treat for my brother, sister and I, and it served to pacify us while we eagerly awaited the finished pie!

Note: Both of these recipes are easy to make so don't be afraid to try making pie crust from scratch!

Mom's Pie Crust

2	cups sifted all-purpose flour
1	teaspoon salt
½	cup Wesson oil
¼	cup cold milk

Preheat oven to 425°. In a large mixing bowl, sift together the flour and salt. In a glass measuring cup measure the milk, add the Wesson oil, and stir until combined. Pour into bowl of dry ingredients and stir with a fork until combined. Roll out on wax paper to fit pie pan. Brown 8-12 minutes.

Yield: 2, 8-inch pie crusts

Note: Many of my pie pans are 9-inch or deep dish, so I use this recipe for one pie crust and use the extra dough for decorative edges.

All Purpose Pie Crust

(Great for pies, cobblers or chicken pot pie!)

2	cups sifted all-purpose flour
1	teaspoon salt
⅔	cup shortening
7	tablespoons <u>cold</u> water

Sift flour and salt together. Using a pastry blender, cut in shortening until pieces are the size of small peas. Sprinkle water over mixture and gently toss with fork until all dry ingredients are moistened. Shape into 2 balls. Roll out on lightly floured surface and follow recipe instructions for cobbler, pot pie, or dessert pie.

Daddy's Apple Pie

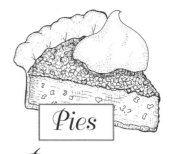

2	9-inch circles of pie crust dough
4	Jonagold apples peeled, cored and thinly sliced
1	teaspoon cinnamon
1	cup sugar
1	tablespoon flour
¼	cup butter, sliced

Toss sliced apples in cinnamon and sugar until evenly coated. Place dough in a 9-inch pie plate, press to fit and trim off extra around edge. Sprinkle flour in bottom of pie shell then pour in apples. Dot apples with slices of butter. Create edge and top crust by overlapping leaf shapes cut out of the second circle of dough. Mini leaf cookie cutters come in very handy for this task. Be sure and moisten the bottom of the leaves with water before you apply them around the edge, overlapping as you go. Bake in a preheated 450° oven for 10 minutes. Put on a pie crust shield or cover the edges with foil. Reduce heat to 350° and bake an additional 35 to 40 minutes or until golden brown. Serve warm.

Note: While making the top crust out of leaf shaped dough makes a beautiful pie, time may not allow you to do so. Your pie will be just as delicious if you simply cover the apples with the second circle of pie dough. Remember to wet and crimp the edges to seal the juices in and cut vents in the top crust to let the steam escape.

Dell and Kaitlyn enjoy making this pie together. It is one of Kaitlyn's favorite father-daughter projects. Plus we all get to enjoy the results!

Time-Saving Tip: Invest in an apple peeler-corer. This neat gadget does the work for you and really saves a lot of time.

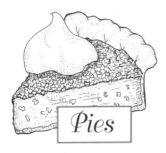

Pies

*T*his pie is great any way you serve it... warm topped with ice cream, room temperature topped with whipped cream, or just plain. It is delicious!

Brownie Pie

1	(12-ounce) package semi-sweet chocolate chips
4	eggs, lightly beaten
2	cups sugar
1	cup flour
1½	teaspoons baking powder
½	teaspoon salt
2	sticks butter, melted
2	teaspoons vanilla
2	cups chopped pecans
2	9-inch unbaked deep dish pie shells

Preheat oven to 350°. Melt chocolate chips in microwave safe bowl for 2 minutes; stir until all chips are melted. Stir in beaten eggs and sugar. Add flour, baking powder, and salt; mix well. Stir in melted butter, vanilla, and pecans. Spoon into pie crusts. Bake for 30 minutes.

Yield: 2, 9-inch pies

German Chocolate Pie

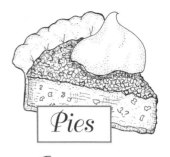

2	9-inch pie shells
1	(4-ounce) package German sweet chocolate
1	stick butter
1	(12-ounce) can evaporated milk
1½	cups sugar
3	tablespoons cornstarch
⅛	teaspoon salt
3	eggs
1	teaspoon vanilla
1½	cups coconut
1	cup chopped pecans

A rich blend of chocolate, coconut, and pecans. This pie is quick, easy to make, and delicious!

Melt chocolate and butter over low heat. Remove from heat and gradually stir in evaporated milk. Set aside. Mix sugar, cornstarch, and salt together in a mixing bowl. Beat in eggs, chocolate mixture, and vanilla. Add coconut and pecans. Pour into pie shells. Bake at 350° for 35 to 40 minutes or until top is crisp and puffed. The filling will be gooey but will set up after pie has cooled 3 to 4 hours.

Yield: 2 pies, 16 servings

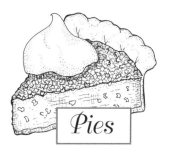

Pies

*A*nother one of my favorites! My mom, Jeanette West, is known for her good pies. Every bite of this delicious pie brings back memories!

For Coconut Cream Pie, top with whipped cream and toasted coconut. Chill before serving.

To toast coconut: Spread in a single layer on a baking sheet with sides. Bake at 325°, stirring occasionally, for 8 to 10 minutes, or until golden brown.

Coconut Meringue Pie

1	9-inch pie shell, baked
¾	cup sugar
⅓	cup plus 1 tablespoon flour
¼	teaspoon salt
2	cups milk
3	eggs, separated
1	tablespoon butter
1	teaspoon vanilla
1½	cups flaked coconut, divided

Combine sugar, flour, and salt in a saucepan. Separate eggs; set whites aside for meringue. Beat egg yolks; blend with milk. Gradually stir into dry ingredients; blend until smooth. Cook stirring constantly over medium heat until mixture thickens. Remove from heat; stir in butter, vanilla, and 1 cup of coconut. Pour into cooled, baked pie shell. Make meringue and spread on top of pie. Sprinkle with ½ cup of coconut. Bake at 350° for 10 to 15 minutes. Cool.

Meringue:

3	egg whites
6	tablespoons sugar
¼	teaspoon cream of tartar

Beat egg whites, gradually adding sugar and cream of tartar. Continue beating until egg whites form stiff peaks. Top pie with meringue. Note: For the best results, make sure your custard has cooled to room temperature and that you spread meringue to the edges of the crust (this will help keep your pie from weeping). Brown in a 350° oven for 10 to 15 minutes or until lightly browned. Cool completely before serving.

Lemon Chess Pie

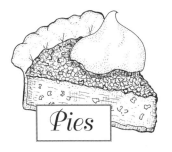

¼	cup butter, softened
2	cups sugar
4	eggs
1	tablespoon flour
1	tablespoon cornmeal
¼	cup milk
¼	cup lemon juice
4	teaspoons grated lemon rind
1	9-inch unbaked pie shell

Cream butter and sugar together; beat in eggs one at a time. Mix in flour and cornmeal; mix well. Add milk, lemon juice, and lemon rind. Pour into an unbaked pie crust and bake for 45 to 50 minutes at 350°.

My father-in-law, Otis Cannon, loved sweets until the day he died, but he especially loved pie. He always said that he never saw a bad piece of pie! This lemon chess recipe was his absolute favorite.

Coconut Chess Pie

1	9-inch unbaked pie crust
3	eggs, beaten
1½	cups sugar
2	tablespoons flour
¼	cup butter, softened
1	cup milk
1	teaspoon vanilla
1	(7-ounce) can flake coconut

This variation is filled with the sweet taste of coconut.

Mix together eggs, sugar, flour, and butter; beat well. Add milk and vanilla. Pour coconut into unbaked pie shell; break any clumps apart with a fork and evenly scatter coconut. Pour mixture over coconut. Bake at 325° for 45 to 50 minutes until golden brown.

169

Pies

$\mathcal{E}$veryone's favorite, this pie is especially refreshing on a hot summer evening.

For a change of pace use crushed vanilla wafers to make the crust. To make crust: Combine 1½ cups of crushed vanilla wafers (about 28 to 30 wafers) with 4 tablespoons of softened butter and 1 tablespoon of sugar. Blend together and press into bottom and sides of pie pan. (To help make your crust smooth and even; place a slightly smaller pie pan on top of your crumb crust and press down.) Bake at 350° for 8 to 10 minutes. Cool before filling.

Granny's Creamy Lemon Pie

1	(8 or 9-inch) graham cracker crust
1	(14-ounce) can sweetened condensed milk
½	cup lemon juice
2	eggs, separated
1½	teaspoons grated lemon rind or ¼ teaspoon lemon extract

Blend sweetened condensed milk, lemon juice, egg yolks, and lemon rind or extract until creamy. Pour into pie crust. Top with meringue.

Meringue:

3	egg whites
6	tablespoons sugar
¼	teaspoon cream of tartar

Beat egg whites, gradually adding sugar, and cream of tartar. Continue beating until egg whites form stiff peaks. Top pie with meringue. Note: For the best results, make sure your custard has cooled to room temperature and that you spread meringue to the edges of the crust (this will help keep your pie from weeping). Bake at 325° for approximately 15 minutes or until meringue is golden brown. Cool, then chill before serving.

Graham Cracker Crust: Combine 1⅔ cup crushed graham crackers with ¼ cup sugar and ¼ cup plus 2 tablespoons of melted butter. Mix well and firmly press into pie pan. Bake at 350° for 7 to 9 minutes. Cool before filling.

Mom's Lemon Meringue Pie

1½	cups sugar
½	cup flour
dash	salt
3	egg yolks
2	tablespoons milk
1½	cups hot water
2	tablespoons butter or margarine
⅓	cup lemon juice
1	teaspoon lemon flavoring
1	(9-inch) pie shell, baked

Combine sugar, flour, and salt. Beat egg yolks with milk. Gradually add to dry mixture along with hot water; stirring constantly. Cook mixture over medium heat continuing to stir until mixture begins to boil. Reduce heat and continue to cook until mixture thickens. Remove from heat. Add butter, lemon juice, and lemon flavoring; stir until smooth and creamy. Pour into baked pie shell and top with meringue. Bake at 350° for 12 to 15 minutes.

Yield: 6-8 servings

Note: For meringue recipe see page 170.

Mom says this is one of her most popular pies. She remembers making them for "Supper Club." Supper clubs were very popular in the late 50's. My parents were in one with several other young married couples from their church. Not only was it a great way to get to know each other, but everyone helped prepare the meal. The hostess provided the main dish and the other couples brought the rest, from salad to dessert.

This is one of my Dad's favorite pies!

Pies

My mom always makes two pecan pies at a time because they are a family favorite. She also says it's just as easy to make two as it is one. Plus, if you make two, you can freeze one or share one with a friend.

Making this pie with finely chopped pecans, like my mother does, makes a very attractive pie. It also cuts into nicer pieces.

You can use a ready made or refrigerated pie crust, but it won't taste as good as mom's!

Mom's Pecan Pie

1	cup sugar
2	heaping tablespoons flour
4	eggs, beaten
1	stick margarine or butter, melted
2	teaspoons vanilla
2	cups light corn syrup
2	cups finely chopped pecans
2	(8-inch) unbaked pie shells

Combine sugar and flour; stir in beaten eggs, melted butter, and vanilla. Mix in corn syrup and stir until mixture is well blended. Sprinkle ½ cup of pecans in the bottom of each pie shell. Pour in pie mixture. Top each pie with an additional ½ cup of chopped pecans. Use a spoon or spatula and gently press pecans into top of pie. Bake slowly at 275° for 1 hour or until golden brown and filling is "set." Cool completely before serving.

Yield: 2, 8-inch pies

Crunchy Raisin Pie

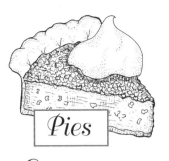

2	cups raisins
4	eggs, separated
1	cup granulated sugar
1	cup brown sugar
2	tablespoons butter
3	tablespoons vinegar
1	teaspoon cinnamon
1	teaspoon allspice
1	teaspoon cloves
1	teaspoon nutmeg
2	unbaked pie shells

Sprinkle 1 cup raisins in each pie shell. Beat egg yolks; add remaining ingredients except egg whites and mix well. Beat egg whites until very stiff and fold in gently. Spoon into unbaked pie shells on top of raisins. Bake at 325° for 45 minutes or until top is brown and crunchy.

Yield: 2, 9-inch pies

Looking for a new and different pie to bake? This unique raisin pie has a great spicy flavor!

Pies

*N*othing reminds me of Thanksgiving more than this classic pumpkin pie. It is always a favorite!

Helpful Hint: To keep children happy and busy while they wait for the Thanksgiving meal, have them make colorful place mats or place cards. Another idea is to have each child write down what they are thankful for and then have them read it at the dinner table.

Classic Pumpkin Pie

1	9-inch deep-dish pie crust, unbaked
2	eggs
¾	cup granulated sugar
½	teaspoon salt
1	teaspoon cinnamon
½	teaspoon ginger
¼	teaspoon ground cloves
1	(16-ounce) can pumpkin
1	(12-ounce) can evaporated milk

Preheat oven to 425°. Beat eggs; add sugar, salt, and spices; mix well. Stir in pumpkin; pour in evaporated milk and mix until smooth. Pour into unbaked pie shell and bake for 15 minutes in a 425° oven. Reduce oven to 350° and bake an additional 40 to 50 minutes. Cool.

Yield: 1, 9-inch pie

Pumpkin Chiffon Pie

A Thanksgiving tradition around the Cannon house!

1	9-inch pie crust, baked
1	package Knox gelatin
¼	cup cold water
3	egg yolks
1	cup sugar, divided
1	(15-ounce) can pumpkin
½	cup milk
½	teaspoon salt
½	teaspoon nutmeg
½	teaspoon cinnamon
½	teaspoon ginger
3	egg whites

Pies

*T*his pie is really not as difficult as it may sound. It is one that is best made at least a day before so the filling is completely chilled. For a special Thanksgiving pie, decorate the edge of your pie crust with leaf designs made with mini cookie cutters. Remember, if you don't want to make your own pie crust, use the refrigerated kind. The filling of this pie is so smooth and delicious, no one will care if you made the pie crust from scratch or not!

Stir packet of gelatin into cold water; set aside. Combine egg yolks, ½ cup sugar, pumpkin, milk, salt, and spices in double boiler. Cook over boiling water, stirring constantly until mixture thickens. Stir in gelatin and continue stirring until it has dissolved and is well blended. Remove from heat. Chill until mixture slightly thickens. Beat egg whites until frothy; gradually add remaining ½ cup sugar, beating until stiff peaks form. Fold egg whites into chilled pumpkin mixture. Return mixture to refrigerator (be sure and cover bowl with plastic wrap or put in an airtight container) until you are ready to serve the pie. Just before serving, pour mixture into baked pie shell. Top each slice with a dollop of whipped cream or whipped topping and a dash of cinnamon.

Yield: 1, 9-inch pie

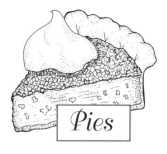

Pies

*A*n easy pie to make, this pie is pretty and delicious! It is best when made with fresh strawberries.

Note: Wash the strawberries just before preparing the pie. They tend to absorb water so wash quickly and drain well on paper towels.

Strawberry Pie

1	9-inch pie crust, baked
2½	cups whole strawberries, washed (cut large ones in half)
¾	cup sugar
2½	tablespoons corn starch
2	tablespoons corn syrup
1	cup water
2	tablespoons strawberry jello
¼	teaspoon red food coloring
1	(8-ounce) carton whipped topping

Cover bottom of pie crust with strawberries. Combine sugar, corn starch, corn syrup, and water in a saucepan. Bring to a boil then remove from heat. Add jello and food coloring; stir until jello is dissolved. Cool, then pour over strawberries in pie crust. Cover with whipped topping and chill in refrigerator.

Note: For an attractive pie use whole strawberries and place them top side down covering bottom of the pie crust. Leave off the whipped topping. Chill completely. To serve, slice and top with a dollop of whipped topping and a sprig of mint.

Chocolate Chip Cookies
"The very best recipe"

1	cup shortening
⅓	cup margarine
1	cup sugar
1	cup brown sugar
2	eggs
2	teaspoons vanilla
3½	cups sifted flour
1	teaspoon soda
½	teaspoon salt
1	(12-ounce) package of semi-sweet chocolate chips
1	cup coarsely chopped pecans

Cream shortening, margarine, and sugars until creamy. Add eggs and vanilla, mix well. Combine flour, soda, and salt; add to creamed mixture. Mix slowly until thoroughly combined. Stir in chocolate chips and pecans. (This may require stirring by hand because this is a thick dough.) Drop by spoonfuls onto a lightly greased (spray with nonstick cooking spray) cookie sheet. Bake in a preheated 375° oven for 8 to 10 minutes until lightly brown. Do not let these get too brown. They should be browned around the edges but still a little gooey in the middle. They will firm up as they cool.

*C*hocolate chip cookies were the first thing I remember my Mom teaching me to bake. They happen to be my most favorite cookie too! Over the years my sister and I have perfected this recipe. It is one of the most popular cookies we make. In fact when I was in high school, several of my friends listed my chocolate chip cookies as their "favorite food" in our school newspaper!

177

Grandmother's Molasses Cookies

*T*his old-fashioned favorite has been updated to save time. If you want cookies that are uniform in size and shape, simply use a cookie scoop to measure out your dough.

1	cup margarine or butter
2	cups sugar
2	eggs, beaten
⅔	cup molasses
4 ½	cups sifted flour
1	teaspoon salt
4	teaspoons soda
2	teaspoons cinnamon
1	teaspoon ginger
1	teaspoon ground cloves
½	cup sugar
½	teaspoon cinnamon

Cream margarine and sugar. Beat in eggs and molasses. Combine flour and spices, slowly add to creamed mixture and mix well. Chill dough for 2 hours. Combine sugar and cinnamon in a small bowl. Shape dough into balls the size of small walnuts, roll in cinnamon/sugar mixture. Place on ungreased cookie sheet and bake in a preheated 350° oven for 10 to 12 minutes. Store in an air tight container.

Yield: 4 dozen cookies

1-18-66

Mary Jane's Oatmeal Cookies

1	cup shortening
1	cup brown sugar
1	cup sugar
2	eggs, beaten
2	tablespoons water
1	teaspoon vanilla
1½	cups flour
1	teaspoon soda
1	teaspoon salt
3	cups 3-minute oats

Cream shortening and sugars. Add eggs, water, and vanilla; mix well. Add flour, soda and salt; mix well then slowly stir in oats. Drop by rounded teaspoon on a lightly greased cookie sheet and bake in a preheated 350° oven for 8 to 10 minutes.

Yield: 3 dozen cookies

Note: For best results, use an air cushion cookie sheet.

I'm always in search of a perfect cookie recipe, one that looks pretty and tastes great. I'd been working on oatmeal cookies for several years when I walked into my dear friend, Paula Johnson's kitchen. There sat a plate of the best looking oatmeal cookies! After tasting them, I knew this was the recipe! Paula told me that it was her mother's recipe and that she had been working to perfect it for years. Well, Mary Jane, you've done it! They are crunchy on the outside and chewy on the inside, just right! Special thanks to Paula and her mother, Mary Jane McClellan.

179

Cookies

*N*othing warms the heart and the kitchen like the smell of cinnamon and cookies baking in the oven.

Mom's Snickerdoodles

1	cup shortening
1½	cups sugar
2	eggs
2 ¾	cups sifted all-purpose flour
½	teaspoon salt
1	teaspoon soda
2	teaspoons cream of tartar
2	teaspoons cinnamon
2	tablespoons sugar

Cream shortening and sugar. Add eggs and mix thoroughly. Combine sifted flour, salt, soda, and cream of tartar; add to first mixture. Mix well then chill dough for several hours. Combine cinnamon and sugar in a small bowl; set aside. When thoroughly chilled, roll dough into balls the size of a small walnut. Roll balls in cinnamon and sugar mixture. Place about 2 inches apart on an ungreased baking sheet. (I like to use the air cushion type.) Bake in a preheated 400° oven for 8 to 10 minutes until lightly browned but still soft.

Yield: 3 to 4 dozen cookies

Sugar Cookies

1	cup butter
1	cup shortening
1	cup powdered sugar
1	cup granulated sugar
2	eggs
4	cups sifted flour
1	teaspoon cream of tartar
1	teaspoon soda
1	teaspoon cinnamon (optional)
1	teaspoon vanilla

These cookies are light and delicious. The best sugar cookies I have ever tasted. For the best results, don't overcook!

In a large mixing bowl, cream butter and shortening until fluffy. Slowly add sugars. Cream thoroughly after each addition. Beat in eggs. Combine sifted flour, cream of tartar, soda, and cinnamon. Add flour mixture slowly; mix well. Stir in vanilla. Chill dough for several hours. When dough is thoroughly chilled, work with ¼ of dough at a time and shape into balls the size of small walnuts. Place on lightly greased cookie sheets. (I prefer using the air cushion type cookie sheets for this recipe.) Coat the bottom of a glass with vegetable oil, dip in granulated sugar and flatten each cookie. Bake in a preheated 350° oven for 8 to 10 minutes or until <u>lightly</u> brown around the edges.

Yield: 4 dozen cookies

Cookies

*S*imple to make using a cake mix. These cookies are simply delicious!

Helpful Hint: Using a cookie scoop gives you a consistent size and a pretty shape. If you do not have a cookie scoop use a metal measuring spoon that is deep and round.

Cake Mix Cookies

¾	cup vegetable oil
1	egg
1	teaspoon vanilla
¼	cup brown sugar
½	cup finely chopped pecans
1	(18-ounce) package yellow or white cake mix

Combine oil, egg, and vanilla; add sugar and beat well. Stir pecans into cake mix and add to sugar mixture. Mix well. Drop by teaspoonfuls (use a cookie scoop) on to a lightly greased cookie sheet. Bake in a preheated 375° oven for 8 to 10 minutes.

Almond Cake Mix Cookies

¾	cup vegetable oil
1	egg
1	teaspoon almond flavoring
¼	cup brown sugar
¾	cup sliced almonds
1	(18-ounce) Duncan Hines Moist Deluxe White Cake Mix

Combine oil, egg, and almond flavoring. Add sugar and mix well. Stir almonds into cake mix; add to sugar mixture. Mix well. Using a tablespoon-size cookie scoop, drop onto lightly greased cookie sheet. Bake in a preheated 375° oven for 8 to 10 minutes until lightly brown. If you would like a smaller cookie use the teaspoon size scoop.

Sand Tarts

1	cup cold butter, sliced
4	heaping tablespoons sifted powdered sugar
2	teaspoons vanilla
2	cups sifted flour
1	tablespoon cold water
1	cup finely chopped pecans

Cream butter and powdered sugar; add vanilla. Alternately add sifted flour and cold water; mix well. Stir in pecans. Chill dough for an hour. Shape dough into crescent shapes or small balls. Place on an air cushion baking sheet that has been lightly greased. Bake at 325° for 15 to 20 minutes. Roll in powdered sugar while still warm and again once cookies have cooled.

Granny's No-Bake Oatmeal Cookies

2	cups sugar
3	tablespoons cocoa
⅓	cup butter
½	cup milk
	dash of salt
½	cup peanut butter
2½	cups 1-minute oatmeal

Combine first 5 ingredients in a saucepan. Bring to a boil and cook for one minute, stirring constantly. Remove from heat and stir in peanut butter and oatmeal. Drop by spoonfuls onto wax paper; let cool.

A classic, these are one of my favorites! This is one recipe where you must use butter. Substituting margarine will alter the results.

When I taste one of these, it reminds me of summers spent on my grandparent's farm in Arkansas. I can still picture Granny making these cookies. My brother Glenn liked the cookies so much he could hardly wait for them to cool. Instead, he just grabbed a spoon and scooped them off the wax paper eating them by the spoonful!

183

4 - 11 - 06

Peanut Butter Cookies

A perfect peanut butter cookie...crispy on the outside and chewy on the inside! This is another recipe children enjoy making. Cookies are a great first-time baking project.

1	cup shortening
1	cup brown sugar
1	cup sugar
2	eggs, beaten
1	teaspoon vanilla
1	cup peanut butter
3	cups flour
2	teaspoons soda
½	teaspoon salt

Cream shortening and sugars. Add eggs and vanilla; beat well. Stir in peanut butter; mix well. Combine flour, soda, and salt. Slowly add flour mixture to creamed mixture, mixing well after each addition. Roll into small balls and place on ungreased air cushion cookie sheet; flatten with fork by making crisscross marks on top. Bake in a preheated 375° oven 8 to 10 minutes until lightly brown. Do not overcook.

Yield: 4 dozen cookies

Vanilla Chip Chocolate Cookies

1	cup butter, softened
1	cup brown sugar
¾	cup sugar
2	eggs, beaten
2	teaspoons vanilla
2⅓	cups sifted all-purpose flour
¾	cup sifted unsweetened cocoa powder
1	teaspoon soda
¼	teaspoon salt
1	(10-ounce) package vanilla chips
1	cup coarsely chopped pecans (optional)

Cream butter and sugars until creamy. Add eggs and vanilla; beat well. Combine flour, cocoa, soda, and salt. Gradually stir into creamed mixture. Stir in vanilla chips and pecans. Drop by teaspoonfuls onto lightly greased baking sheet. Bake in a preheated 375° oven for 9 to 11 minutes. Do not overbake. Cool slightly before removing from cookie sheet.

Yield: 4 dozen cookies

This is a wonderful combination of flavors and a new family favorite!

Hint: These cookies will still look soft when you take them out of the oven, but do not overbake. If you do, they will be too hard after they have cooled.

Peanut Butter Blossoms

1	cup sugar
1	cup brown sugar
1	cup margarine
1	cup peanut butter
2	eggs
¼	cup milk
2	teaspoons vanilla
3½	cups flour
2	teaspoons baking soda
1	teaspoon salt
2	(10-ounce) packages chocolate kisses

*B*e sure and have the chocolate kisses unwrapped so they are ready when the cookies come out of the oven. Or to save time, they now have packages of unwrapped mini chocolate kisses. If you use these, place 3 mini kisses in the center of each cookie.

Note: I have frozen these, but they are best warm just out of the oven!

Cream sugars, margarine, and peanut butter until fluffy. Mix in eggs, milk, and vanilla. Combine flour, baking soda, and salt. Stir into creamed mixture; mix well. Roll into balls the size of a small walnut and roll in granulated sugar. Place on an ungreased cookie sheet and bake in a preheated 375° oven for 10 to 12 minutes. Immediately press in a chocolate kiss.

Yield: 4 dozen cookies

Candy Cane Cookies

½	cup shortening
½	cup butter or margarine, softened
1	cup sifted powdered sugar
1	egg
1½	teaspoons almond extract
1	teaspoon vanilla
2½	cups sifted all-purpose flour
½	teaspoon salt
½	teaspoon red food coloring

Mix together shortening, butter, powdered sugar, egg, and flavorings. When creamy, gradually add flour and salt. Mix well. Divide dough in half. Add red food coloring to one half, stir until coloring is blended in. Chill dough for 1 hour. Roll a teaspoonful of each color into a 4 inch piece about the size of a pencil. Twist together and place on an ungreased air cushion cookie sheet. Curve top down to resemble a candy cane. In a preheated 375° oven, bake approximately 9 minutes or until lightly brown. Remove while warm and sprinkle with sugar or crushed peppermint candy if desired.

Yield: 4 dozen cookies

*C*andy Cane Cookies are a Christmas tradition around our house. My Mom first made them when I was a little girl and now I make them for my kids. They are always a favorite at a holiday cookie exchange or school Christmas parties.

Cookies

*W*hen my son, Logan, was in fifth grade, I made brownies for his class and quickly became "famous" for my brownies. His teacher, Kendra Head and her husband Darren said they were the best brownies they had ever tasted! So, of course, I always brought extra brownies for Darren and Kendra!

Note: These brownies are so rich they do not need icing.

Susan's Saucepan Brownies
"Easy to make and richly delicious!"

4	ounces unsweetened chocolate squares
⅔	cup butter
2	cups sugar
4	eggs
2	teaspoons vanilla
1	cup flour
1	teaspoon baking powder
¾	teaspoon salt
1½	cups coarsely chopped pecans

In a saucepan over low heat melt chocolate and butter. Remove from heat and stir in sugar, eggs, and vanilla. Combine flour, baking powder, and salt; stir into chocolate mixture. Continue stirring until mixture is thoroughly combined. Stir in pecans. Pour into a 9x13-inch glass baking dish that has been sprayed with nonstick cooking spray. Bake in a preheated 350° oven for 20 to 25 minutes. Let cool and cut into squares.

Brownie Sundae

Place a scoop of vanilla ice cream on a saucepan brownie warm from the oven. Cover ice cream and brownie with hot fudge sauce (page 208) and chopped pecans. Enjoy!

Brownies
With Chocolate Icing

2	cups sugar
1	cup shortening
4	eggs
2	tablespoons corn syrup
1½	cups flour
⅔	cup cocoa
½	teaspoon salt
2	teaspoons vanilla
1	cup chopped pecans

Cream sugar and shortening; add eggs and corn syrup. Combine flour, cocoa, and salt. Mix into creamed mixture. Stir in vanilla and pecans. Pour into a greased 9x13 pan. Bake in a preheated 350° oven for 25 to 30 minutes. Cool and then spread with icing.

Icing:

4 ½	tablespoons margarine
7 ½	tablespoons sugar
3	tablespoons milk
½	teaspoon vanilla
¼	cup semi-sweet chocolate chips

Combine margarine, sugar, and milk in a saucepan. Bring to a boil and boil for 3 minutes. Remove from heat. Beat 2 minutes and then stir in vanilla and chocolate chips. Beat until it thickens then pour over brownies.

Brownies are a favorite among my children and their friends. I always take them to their class parties at school.

Try these variations: For Valentines, cut brownies into heart shapes with a cookie cutter and sprinkle with mini M&Ms.

For Christmas, cut into tree shapes (you can leave the chocolate icing off). Create a garland on the tree with colored icing and decorate with mini M&Ms.

Cookies

*A*nother quick and easy favorite! These bar cookies are filled with so many good flavors including coconut, oatmeal, chocolate chips, and pecans!

Store in an airtight container to keep these fresh.

Goody Bars

½	cup margarine, softened
1	cup brown sugar
1	egg
1	teaspoon vanilla
1¼	cups flour
½	teaspoon baking soda
½	teaspoon salt
1	cup quick-cooking oats, uncooked
½	cup coconut
¾	cup semi-sweet chocolate chips
½	cup chopped pecans

Cream margarine and sugar. Mix in egg and vanilla. Combine flour, baking soda, and salt. Add to creamed mixture and mix well. Stir in oats and coconut. Add chocolate chips and pecans; stir until combined. Pour into a lightly greased 9x13-inch glass pan. Bake in a preheated 375° oven for 20 minutes. Cool and cut into bars.

Yield: 12 to 15 cookies

Cookies

Peanut Butter Oatmeal Bars

½	cup shortening
½	cup sugar
½	cup brown sugar
⅓	cup peanut butter
½	teaspoon vanilla
1	egg
¼	cup milk
1	cup sifted all-purpose flour
½	teaspoon baking soda
½	teaspoon salt
1	cup quick cooking oats, uncooked

These take a little extra time but are worth the effort. A wonderful blending of flavors; oatmeal, peanut butter, and chocolate ... Yum!

Cream shortening, sugars, peanut butter, and vanilla until fluffy. Add egg and milk; beat well. Combine flour, baking soda, and salt; add to creamed mixture; mix just until well combined. Stir in oats. Spread evenly in a 9x13-inch glass pan that has been sprayed with nonstick cooking spray. Bake in a preheated 350° oven for 20 minutes. Cool completely.

Icing:

2	cups sifted powdered sugar
¼	cup cocoa
½	cup butter, melted
3	tablespoons boiling water
½	teaspoon vanilla

In a mixing bowl, sift together powdered sugar and cocoa. Quickly stir in melted butter, boiling water and vanilla. Beat until smooth. Spread over cooled cookies. Drizzle with the glaze.

Glaze:

2	tablespoons butter, melted
1	cup powdered sugar
	3 to 4 teaspoons milk

Combine all ingredients; stir until smooth. Pour glaze into a plastic bag. Snip off one corner to make a tiny hole. Drizzle glaze over cookies. Cool and cut into bars.

191

Cookies

German Chocolate Brownies

*R*ich brownies
filled with butterscotch
chips, caramel, and
pecans. Quick and
easy!

1	(18.25) package German Chocolate cake mix
¾	cup margarine, melted
⅔	cup evaporated milk, divided
1	(6-ounce) package butterscotch chips
1	cup chopped pecans
1	(4-ounce) package caramels

Note: You can melt the caramels in the microwave. Place in a microwave-safe bowl and heat on high 2 to 3 minutes. Stirring after each minute.

Combine dry cake mix, melted margarine, and ⅓ cup evaporated milk in a large mixing bowl. Stir by hand until combined; dough will be thick. Press ½ of dough into a lightly greased 9x13-inch pan. Bake for 8 minutes in a preheated 350° oven. While first part is cooking, heat caramels and remaining ⅓ cup evaporated milk in a double boiler, stir occasionally until caramels are completely melted. Remove baked mixture from oven and sprinkle with butterscotch chips and pecans. Next pour on melted caramels. Spread remaining dough on top. Bake an additional 20 minutes at 350°. Do not overbake. It will look gooey but let it set for one hour, then cut into small squares.

Yield: 24 cookies

Sinfully Rich Devil's Food Brownies

1	(18.25-ounce) package Duncan Hines Devil's Food cake mix
1	stick margarine or butter, melted
¾	cup creamy peanut butter
1	(7-ounce) jar marshmallow creme
1	cup chopped pecans

Combine dry cake mix and melted butter. Press half of mixture into an ungreased 9x13-inch pan. Combine peanut butter and marshmallow creme then spread on top of dough mixture. Sprinkle pecans evenly over second layer. Crumble remaining mixture on top. Bake in a preheated 350° oven for 20 minutes. They will look gooey but let them set for 1 hour before drizzling with icing. Cut into squares.

Chocolate Icing:

2	tablespoons cocoa
¼	cup margarine
¼	cup milk
½	teaspoon vanilla
2	cups powdered sugar

Combine cocoa, margarine, and milk in a saucepan. Bring to a boil, add vanilla. Remove from heat and stir in powdered sugar.

Another delicious brownie recipe. It is quick and easy!

Note: I often melt the margarine or butter in the microwave. If once you have added it to the cake mix the mixture seems too dry and crumbly simply add an additional tablespoon or two of melted margarine.

Hint: To drizzle icing, spoon icing into a plastic zip-top bag and cut a small hole in one corner. Squeeze to drizzle icing over brownies then for a simple cleanup throw the bag away!

*B*oth of these recipes make a pretty cookie. Their light lemony flavor makes them perfect for teas and showers.

*Q*uick and easy, these light cookies melt in your mouth! Serve with Mint Tea (page 24) on a hot summer day!

Deluxe Lemon Bars

2	cups flour
½	cup powdered sugar
1	cup butter or margarine
4	eggs
2	cups sugar
⅓	cup lemon juice
¼	cup flour
½	teaspoon baking powder

Combine flour, powdered sugar, and butter; mix well. Press into the bottom of a 9x13-inch glass baking dish that has been sprayed with nonstick cooking spray. Bake in a preheated 350° oven for 20 to 25 minutes. Cream eggs, sugar, and lemon juice until creamy. Fold in ¼ cup flour and baking powder. Pour over crust. Bake at 350° for 25 minutes. Cool well, cut into squares, and dust with sifted powdered sugar.

Lemon Delights

1	(18-ounce) box lemon cake mix
1	(8-ounce) container whipped topping
2	eggs
1	cup powdered sugar

Combine cake mix, thawed whipped topping, and eggs. Mix well. Shape into balls; roll in powdered sugar. Place on an ungreased cookie sheet approximately 2 inches apart. Bake at 350° for 8 to 10 minutes or until lightly golden .

Apricot Bars

¾	cup margarine
1	cup sugar
2	cups flour, sifted
¾	teaspoon of salt
½	teaspoon soda
1	cup chopped pecans
1½	cups angel flake coconut
1	(16-ounce) jar apricot preserves

Preheat oven to 400°. Cream together margarine and sugar. Add dry ingredients (mixture will be crumbly). Mix in nuts and coconut. Press 4 cups of mixture into the bottom of a 9x13-inch glass baking dish that has been sprayed with nonstick cooking spray. Bake for 10 to 12 minutes. Remove from oven. Spoon on preserves and crumble remaining mixture on top. Bake again for 20 minutes or until golden brown. Let cool then cut into squares.

Yield: 15 cookies

My husband loves apricots and this is one of his favorites! This recipe was given to us by my cousin, Rosemary West.

For variety try your favorite preserve like peach or cherry!

*R*ich and chewy, these have a great praline taste!

A simple graham cracker is turned into a delicious treat when topped with pecans and a praline glaze. These are quick and easy to make!

Praline Brownies

1	stick butter
2	cups brown sugar
2	eggs
2	tablespoons corn syrup
1	teaspoon vanilla
1¼	cups all-purpose flour
dash	salt
2	cups chopped pecans

Cream butter and brown sugar. Add eggs, corn syrup, and vanilla. Gradually stir in flour and salt; mix well. Stir in pecans. Pour in a greased and floured 9x13-inch pan. Bake in a preheated 350° oven for 25 to 30 minutes. Do not overcook. They will still be gooey in the middle. Cool completely before cutting into squares.

Graham Cracker Praline Cookies

24	graham crackers
1	stick of margarine
1	cup brown sugar
¼	teaspoon vanilla
1	cup finely chopped pecans

Place graham crackers on a baking sheet with sides. Boil margarine and brown sugar in a saucepan for 3 minutes. Remove from heat, add vanilla, and set aside. Sprinkle pecans evenly over graham crackers; pour sugar mixture over crackers. Bake at 350° for 10 minutes. Remove from cookie sheet to foil and let cool; break into fourths.

Grandmother West's Fudge

3	cups semi-sweet chocolate chips
2	(½-ounce) unsweetened chocolate squares
1	(7-ounce) jar marshmallow creme
4½	cups sugar
1	(12-ounce) can evaporated milk
2	sticks butter
pinch	salt
2	teaspoons vanilla
2½	cups coarsely chopped pecans

Spray jellyroll pan with nonstick cooking spray. Place chocolate chips, unsweetened chocolate, and marshmallow cream in a large bowl. Set aside. Bring sugar, evaporated milk, butter, and salt to a boil in a saucepan, stirring constantly at the beginning to keep from sticking. Boil mixture 8 minutes. Pour hot mixture over chocolate and marshmallow creme; stir until all chocolate is melted and mixture is smooth. Stir in vanilla and pecans. Pour out on prepared jelly roll pan. Let cool completely then cut into small squares.

Note from Grandmother West: "This fudge does not harden quickly. I usually make it at night and let it set until morning."

Yield: 5 pounds

*I*f you like fudge, you will absolutely love this recipe. It is smooth and creamy with just the right amount of sweetness. It is also easy to make! One batch makes a lot. You will have enough for your family and plenty to share! Every bite of this creamy fudge brings back memories of Christmas on West Farm!

Candy

*I*f you like peanut butter, you will love this creamy fudge! It is also very easy to make.

Hint: If you are going to make candy, invest in a candy thermometer! It saves a lot of guess-work and frustration!

Note: To make marshmallow creme easier to spoon out remove lid and heat in the microwave for 30 seconds.

Peanut Butter Fudge

3	cups light brown sugar, packed
1	(5-ounce) can evaporated milk
½	cup butter
1	(7-ounce) jar marshmallow creme
1	cup creamy peanut butter
2	teaspoons vanilla

Combine brown sugar, milk, and butter in a 2½ quart saucepan. Stirring constantly, bring to a full boil. Boil until temperature reaches 240° on a candy thermometer. This will take about 5 to 7 minutes. Do not scrape sides of saucepan because it will make your fudge grainy. When mixture has reached 240° remove from heat. Add marshmallow creme, peanut butter, and vanilla; stir until smooth. Spread into a greased 9x13-inch pan. Cool and cut into small squares.

Peanut Brittle

2	cups sugar
1	cup light corn syrup
½	cup water
2	cups raw peanuts
2	teaspoons soda
1	teaspoon vanilla

Combine sugar, corn syrup, water, and peanuts in a heavy sauce pan. Cook over medium-high heat until mixture is boiling and until sugar mixture turns a caramel color, peanuts will turn light brown and begin to crack (300 °on a candy thermometer). Remove from heat; quickly add soda and vanilla. Stir to mix well. Pour out on a greased jelly roll pan. Using a wooden spoon, quickly spread candy out to a ½ inch thickness or less. Once it has hardened break into pieces.

Note: Store in an airtight container.

Peanut brittle, is another candy that I always associate with Christmas and with Naydiene. She always made several batches so as to be sure that there was an ample supply for family and visiting friends. Dell has vivid memories of his mother cooking it to perfection then "hollering" for him to come help her spread it out. A wonderful variation to this recipe comes from Dell's aunt, Mack Cannon. She always put ½ cup of ribbon coconut in her peanut brittle which adds a delightful flavor and texture to this traditional candy.

Candy

A wonderful combination of peanut butter and chocolate! These take a little extra time, but they are worth it. This recipe makes a lot which is a good thing because all the grandkids eat them by the handful!

Peanut Butter Balls

2	cups creamy peanut butter
1	stick butter
3 ¾	cups unsifted powdered sugar

Spoon peanut butter into a large bowl. Melt butter, pour over peanut butter and stir. Pour in powdered sugar and mix well. Knead mixture until smooth. Roll into marble sized balls. Chill completely.

Chocolate Coating:

2	cups chocolate chips
¼	pound paraffin

Melt chocolate chips and paraffin together in a double boiler. Using small tongs, dip balls in melted chocolate mixture. Place on wax paper to cool. When you have dipped all of the candy balls once, dip them again.

Note: I buy peanut butter, powdered sugar, and chocolate chips in bulk, so I listed the ingredient measurements by cups. If you want to buy just what you need for this recipe, you will need:

1	*(18-ounce) jar peanut butter*
1	*(1-pound) box powdered sugar*
1	*(12-ounce) package chocolate chips*

Divinity

2½	cups sugar
½	cup light corn syrup
½	cup water
2	egg whites
1	teaspoon vanilla
½	cup finely chopped pecans

In a heavy 2-quart saucepan combine sugar, syrup, and water. Cook over medium-high heat stirring constantly until mixture is boiling. Clip on candy thermometer. Reduce heat to medium; continue cooking <u>without</u> stirring until the thermometer reaches 260° (hard-ball stage). Remove candy thermometer and remove saucepan from heat. <u>Immediately</u> beat egg whites in a large bowl with electric mixer at medium speed until stiff peaks form. <u>Gradually</u> pour hot mixture in a <u>thin</u> stream over egg whites, beating on high and scraping the bowl occasionally. Add vanilla. Continue beating on high until the candy starts to lose its gloss. A spoonful of mixture dropped on waxed paper should remain mounded. (If candy flattens, beat an additional minute). Stir in nuts. Quickly drop candy from a teaspoon onto waxed paper.

Note: If mixture is too stiff to spoon and is rough in texture, beat in HOT water a few drops at a time until softer.

Yield: 20 pieces

Divinity always reminds me of my Grandmother West. Not that she made divinity, but several other relatives did. They would bring the divinity to my grandmother's house so we could all enjoy it at Christmas. I can see it now... sitting on her buffet in shirt boxes lined with wax paper. Those fluffy white mounds just waiting to be tasted! Jack Parker made the best. This is not her recipe, but it comes pretty close. The key to making divinity is to have patience and choose a warm, dry day. Thankfully, we often have those kind of days here in Texas even in December!

Candy

$\mathcal{M}$y sister and her mother-in-law, Val Franks, get together every Christmas season to make candy. Val is a great candy-maker. My sister, Karen, is a school teacher and gives a plateful of assorted candies to her co-workers and her children's teachers. They look forward to it every year!

Peanut Pralines

2	cups raw spanish peanuts
2	cups sugar
⅛	teaspoon salt
1	(5⅓-ounce) can evaporated milk
½	cup light corn syrup
⅓	cup butter or margarine
1	teaspoon vanilla
10	drops red food coloring

Roast peanuts in 350° oven for 10 minutes or until browned. Combine sugar, salt, milk, and corn syrup in a saucepan. Bring to a boil using medium heat stirring often. Cook stirring continuously to 228° or until a very fine ball is formed in cold water. Remove from heat; add butter, vanilla, and food color. Beat until smooth. Add roasted peanuts and continue beating until mixture is creamy and holds its shape. Drop on waxed paper.

Yield: 30 pralines

Candy

Chocolate Turtles

1	(14-ounce) package caramels
2	tablespoons margarine
3	tablespoons water
2¼	cups pecan halves
2	cups semisweet chocolate chips
⅓	of a ¼ lb. paraffin

Melt caramels, margarine, and water in double boiler. When melted stir in pecans. Remove from heat. Drop by spoonfuls out on a greased cookie sheet. Cool. Melt chocolate chips and paraffin in double boiler; stir well. Dip candy in melted chocolate. Return to cookie sheet to cool. Store in an airtight container.

Filled with caramel and pecans these are always a favorite!

Note: If you prefer you can melt the caramels in your microwave.

Apricot Balls

2	(8-ounce) packages dried apricots, diced
2	(7-ounce) cans flake coconut
2	cups finely chopped pecans
1	(14-ounce) can sweetened condensed milk

Chop apricots into small pieces (If you have one use a food processor). Combine chopped apricots and remaining ingredients in a large bowl; stir until well mixed. Chill for several hours. Roll into bite size balls (this process is a little messy; it helps to dust your hands with powdered sugar). Roll balls in powdered sugar. Store in an airtight container.

Easy to make! No cooking, just mix together and enjoy!

203

Candy

A Texas favorite!
We enjoy pralines year
round, but especially
enjoy making them and
giving them to friends
and family during the
holidays!

Note: To keep pralines
fresh individually wrap
them in plastic wrap.

Note: To be sure you
get a pecan in every
bite use coarsely
chopped pecans or
instead of using a nut
chopper simply break
the pecans into pieces.
Also, some cooks
prefer to use a
combination of pecan
halves and chopped
pecans.

Pecan Pralines

1	cup brown sugar
1	cup white sugar
1	cup light corn syrup
1	(14-ounce) can sweetened condensed milk
2	sticks butter
3	cups pecans, chopped
1	teaspoon vanilla extract

Combine first five ingredients. While stirring constantly, bring to a boil over low heat. Boil until it reaches the soft ball stage (forms a soft ball when dropped into a cup of cold water or reaches 240° on a candy thermometer). Remove from heat; add pecans and vanilla. Stir until mixture is thick, then drop by spoonfuls onto a greased cookie sheet.

Note: For the best results you really need a candy thermometer. It will save a lot of guesswork and frustration!

Also, do not drop onto wax paper, the heat of the candy mixture causes the pralines to stick as they cool.

Apricot Cobbler

4	cups fresh ripe apricots
1¼	cups sugar
2	cups water
2	tablespoons flour
½	teaspoon cinnamon

Wash apricots, pull in half and remove pit. Place in a saucepan with sugar, water, flour, and cinnamon. Bring mixture to a boil and simmer for 10 minutes, stirring occasionally. Set aside.

Crust:

3	cups all-purpose flour
1	teaspoon salt
¾	teaspoon baking powder
¾	cup shortening
8	tablespoons ice water

Combine flour, salt, and baking powder; cut in shortening with pastry blender until it looks like coarse meal. Sprinkle ice water evenly over dry ingredients; stir with a fork until moistened. Shape dough into a ball. Roll ¾ of pastry to ⅛-inch thickness on a lightly floured surface. Fit into a 9x13-inch baking dish that has been lightly sprayed with nonstick cooking spray. Spoon cooked apricots on top of crust. Roll remaining pastry out to ¼-inch thickness and cut into one inch strips. Arrange in a lattice fashion over apricots. Sprinkle lightly with cinnamon/sugar mixture. Bake at 350° for 30 to 40 minutes.

Desserts

In Texas we love cobbler and this one is a favorite!

Note: If fresh apricots are not available, frozen will work just as well. Also you can use refrigerated pie crust, but it will not taste as good as homemade.

Desserts

*A*nother classic family favorite! For an attractive dessert, make your banana pudding in a pretty, clear glass bowl. Finish off the top of the bowl by placing vanilla wafers around the edge leaving half of the wafer showing.

Mom's Banana Pudding

¾	cup sugar
⅓	cup flour
¼	teaspoon of salt (optional)
2¼	cups milk
2	large eggs - yolks only
2	tablespoons butter
1	teaspoon vanilla
15-20	vanilla wafers
3	ripe bananas

Combine sugar, flour, and salt in a saucepan. Blend together milk and egg yolks; gradually stir into flour mixture. Cook over medium heat, stirring constantly, until thickened. Remove from heat; add butter. Let cool slightly; add vanilla and stir. Place a layer of vanilla wafers in a round casserole or glass bowl; top with half of bananas and half of pudding. Repeat layers. Chill before serving.

Cherry Puddin' Pie

1	(16-ounce) can pie cherries
1	teaspoon soda
2	cups sugar
1½	cups flour
2	eggs, beaten
4	tablespoons butter, melted
1	tablespoon red food coloring
1	cup chopped pecans
1	teaspoon vanilla

Drain cherries, save juice and set aside. Stir soda into cherries; let sit. Mix sugar and flour together. Make a well in the middle of the flour mixture and stir in beaten eggs. Add melted butter and red food coloring. Gently stir in pecans and vanilla. Gradually add cherry juice and beat well. Stir in cherries. Mixture will have an odd color. Pour into a 9x13 sheet cake pan and bake at 300° for 40 minutes. Remove from oven and pour sauce over pudding. Refrigerate at least 12 hours. To serve, cut into squares and top with a dollop of whipped cream.

Sauce:

2	cups brown sugar
4	tablespoons flour
pinch	salt
2	tablespoons melted butter
2	cups hot water

Combine all ingredients in a saucepan. Bring the mixture to a boil; reduce heat and cook until it thickens.

My husband, Dell, remembers his mom making this dessert often for guests. Dell and his cousins especially liked it, but couldn't decide if it was a pie or pudding so they nicknamed it Cherry Puddin' Pie!

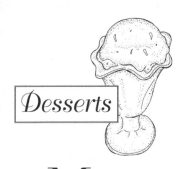

Desserts

*M*y sister's boys often request Fruit Pizza on their birthdays instead of cake.

Note: If using sliced bananas or apples, dip them in lemon juice to keep them from turning brown.

*D*elicious over brownies and ice cream.

Note: Extra sauce may be stored in your refrigerator for several weeks.

Fruit Pizza

1	(18-ounce) package refrigerated sugar cookie dough
1	(8-ounce) package cream cheese, softened
½	cup sugar
½	teaspoon vanilla
	fresh fruit in season, sliced
1	tablespoon apple jelly

Slice cookie dough place on pizza pan and press to fit. Bake according to package directions and let cool. Mix cream cheese, sugar, and vanilla until creamy. Spread on baked cookie crust. Top with assorted sliced fresh fruit arranged in an attractive pattern. Combine apple jelly with enough water (just a little) so it will spread and lightly glaze your pizza. Refrigerate.

Hot Fudge Sauce

¼	cup semi-sweet chocolate chips
1	(1-ounce) square unsweetened chocolate
½	stick butter or margarine
¾	cup sugar
½	cup evaporated milk
½	teaspoon vanilla

Melt chocolate chips, unsweetened chocolate, and butter in a saucepan over low heat. Stir in sugar and evaporated milk. Cook over low heat until thick. Add vanilla.

Caramel Ice Cream Crust

2	cups flour
½	cup brown sugar
½	cup oatmeal
1½	cups chopped pecans
2	sticks butter or margarine
1	(12-ounce) jar caramel sauce
½	gallon vanilla ice cream, softened

Combine first five ingredients mix well. Spread on a cookie sheet lined with foil. Bake at 350° for 30 to 35 minutes or until mixture is nicely browned and nuts are toasted. While mixture is cooking, stir every 10 to 15 minutes so it will be crumbly and toasted throughout. Put half of crust mixture in the bottom of a 9x13-inch pan. Warm jar of caramel sauce and drizzle over crust mixture. Spread softened ice cream on top. Sprinkle with remaining crust mixture. Freeze for at least one hour, cut into squares, and serve.

Yield: 12-15 servings

This easy dessert has a wonderful praline flavor!

Quick Tip: Set the jar of caramel in a bowl of hot water while you prepare crust or remove the lid and microwave on medium just until caramel is warm.

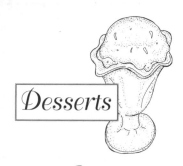

Desserts

A wonderful
combination of cream
cheese, pumpkin, and a
buttery cake crust. It is
delicious!

Time-Saving Tip:
Soften cream cheese in
the microwave. Remove
from foil package, place
in a microwave-safe
bowl and cook at 50%
power for about 1
minute.

Creamy Pumpkin Squares

Crust:

1	(18.5-ounce) package yellow cake mix
1	egg
1	stick butter, melted

Preheat oven to 350°. Pour dry cake mix into a bowl (break up any small lumps); add egg and melted butter; mix well. Press into the bottom of a lightly greased 9x13-inch glass baking dish. Set aside and prepare filling.

Filling:

1	(8-ounce) package cream cheese, softened
2	eggs
1	teaspoon vanilla
1	stick butter, melted
1	(16-ounce) can pumpkin
1	teaspoon cinnamon
¼	teaspoon nutmeg
2	cups powdered sugar

Beat cream cheese until smooth. Add eggs, vanilla, and melted butter; beat until smooth. Add pumpkin and spices; mix well. Gradually add powdered sugar, mixing well. Pour over crust and bake at 350° for about 40 minutes. Do not over bake. The center will be gooey when you take it out of the oven. Let cool completely. Top with a dollop of whipped topping and toasted pecans. Yummy!

Texas Delight

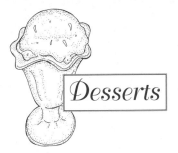

1st layer:

1	cup flour
½	cup margarine
½	cup chopped pecans

Combine all ingredients and press into a 9x13-inch glass dish. Bake at 350° for 15 minutes. Cool completely.

2nd layer:

1	(8-ounce) package cream cheese, softened
½	(10-ounce) carton whipped topping, thawed
1	cup sifted powdered sugar

Mix together and spread over cooled crust.

3rd layer:

2	(3.9-ounce) packages milk chocolate pudding
2½	cups milk

Combine pudding and milk; cook until thick. Cool. Spread on top of cream cheese layer. Spread on remaining whipped topping and garnish with chopped pecans. Chill several hours. Cut into squares.

Yield: 15 servings

This dessert truly is a delight! It is cool, creamy, very rich, and one of our all-time favorites.

Time-Saving Tip: See the tip about softening cream cheese in the microwave on the previous page!

Another summertime favorite from the farm. This ice cream is a favorite of many on both sides of our family.

Helpful Hint: To peel peaches dip in boiling water for 20 to 30 seconds then plunge immediately in cold water. The skin will now peel off easily with the aid of a small paring knife.

Note: If fresh peaches are not available you can use frozen peaches.

Fresh Peach Ice Cream

6	cups fresh peaches, peeled and puréed
1	cup sugar
3	eggs
1½	cups sugar
2	tablespoons all-purpose flour
½	teaspoon salt
1	quart milk
1	cup whipping cream
1	tablespoon vanilla

Combine puréed peaches and 1 cup sugar; stir well and set aside. Beat eggs with mixer until frothy. Combine 1 ½ cups sugar, flour, and salt. Gradually add dry mixture to eggs, beating until thick. Add in milk and mix well. Pour this mixture into a saucepan. Cook over low heat, stirring constantly for approximately 15 minutes or until mixture thickens and coats the spoon. Remove from heat and set in cold water; stir gently until cool. Stir in whipping cream and vanilla. Add peaches and stir well. Pour mixture into a 1 gallon manual or electric freezer. Freeze according to your freezer's instructions. When frozen, remove dasher from can and let the ice cream ripen for at least 1 hour before serving.

Yield: 1 gallon

Note: 4 cups = 1 quart

Coconut Ice Cream

6	eggs, well beaten
1	cup sugar
2	(14-ounce) cans sweetened condensed milk
1	pint half and half
1	(15-ounce) can cream of coconut
½	teaspoon coconut flavoring
2	cups frozen grated coconut

milk (to fill line on freezer can)

Beat eggs well; add sugar and mix well. Add remaining ingredients except milk and mix until well blended. Pour into a 1 gallon freezer can, add milk to fill line. Freeze in a hand crank or electric freezer according to manufacturer's instructions.

Yield: 1-gallon

Note: We have found that the Coco Lopez brand of cream of coconut works best. Many of the others make the ice cream too salty.

*I*f you like coconut, you will love this rich and creamy ice cream!

Note: After ice cream has frozen, allow it to "ripen" packed in ice in the freezer for at least 2 hours. This allows the flavor to fully develop.

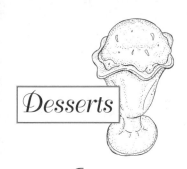

A favorite with kids of all ages! This ice cream is very easy to make and is rich and delicious!

Note: To speed freezing process, chill mixture before pouring into canister.

Butterfinger Ice Cream

6	eggs
3	cups sugar
dash	salt
¼	cup peanut butter
1	pint whipping cream
1	(3-ounce) can evaporated milk
6	(1⁹⁄₁₆-ounce) Butterfinger candies, crushed
milk (to fill line on freezer can)	

Beat eggs until lemon colored; add sugar and salt. Beat until mixture is thick. Stir in peanut butter and vanilla. Add cream and evaporated milk; mix well. Stir in crushed candy. Pour into a 1 gallon electric or manual freezer. Add milk to the freezer's fill line. Freeze according to the manufacturer's instructions. Let ripen for at least 2 hours.

Yield 1-gallon

Petite Cheesecakes

2	(8-ounce) packages cream cheese, softened
¾	cup sugar
2	eggs
1	tablespoon lemon juice
1	teaspoon vanilla
24	vanilla wafers
1	(16-ounce) can cherry pie filling

Beat cream cheese, sugar, eggs, lemon juice, and vanilla until light and fluffy. Line muffin pans with paper baking cups. Put one vanilla wafer in each cup. Fill cups ⅔ full. Bake at 375° for 15 to 20 minutes. Cool. Top with 1 tablespoon cherry pie filling. Chill completely.

These mini cheesecakes are so good you will not believe how easy they are to make! Topped with cherry pie filling or the praline sauce below they are delicious!

Praline Sauce

1	cup light corn syrup
½	cup sugar
⅓	cup butter
1	egg, beaten
1	tablespoon vanilla extract
1	cup coarsely chopped pecans

Combine corn syrup, sugar, butter, and beaten egg in a saucepan. Stir until well combined. Bring to a boil over medium heat, stirring constantly. Boil 2 minutes <u>without</u> stirring. Remove from heat. Stir in vanilla and pecans.

This praline sauce is wonderful, and when combined with cheesecake, makes an outstanding dessert! Use with the recipe above or simply serve warm over slices of store bought cheesecake.

Desserts

$\mathcal{K}$ids of all ages love this old time favorite!

Note: My sister, Karen, advises making a double batch of this recipe because this popular snack goes fast. Plus it keeps well in airtight containers.

Karen's Caramel Corn

9 to 12	cups popped popcorn
1	cup brown sugar packed
½	cup butter or margarine
¼	cup light corn syrup
½	teaspoon salt
½	teaspoon baking soda

Heat oven to 200°. Put popped corn in two 9x13-inch pans that have been sprayed with non-stick cooking spray. Combine brown sugar, butter, corn syrup, and salt in saucepan. Cook over medium heat, stirring constantly until it bubbles around edges. Cook 5 more minutes and take off heat. Add baking soda then stir until it's foamy. Pour sauce over popcorn and stir until popcorn is coated. Bake 1 hour, stirring every 15 minutes. Store in an airtight container.

Note: 1 cup of peanuts sprinkled in with the popcorn before the sauce is poured on, makes a tasty addition!

Hint: The amount of popped popcorn you use determines how sweet the finished product is. For example if you use 12 cups of popped popcorn you will have a lighter coating of caramel. Adjust accordingly to your personal preference.

Index

Index

Index

Index

Index

221

Index

Index

Index

To order additional copies of

"Where Hearts Gather"

call
1-800-533-8983
or
order online at www.whereheartsgather.com